Pursuing Purpose Workbook

5 Keys to Fulfilling Your God-Given Purpose

Pursuing Purpose Workbook

5 Keys to Fulfilling Your God-Given Purpose

Kyra Lanae

GLORIOUS WORKS PUBLISHING
UPPER DARBY, PENNSYLVANIA

Copyright © 2019 by Kyra Lanae

All rights reserved. This book or any portion thereof may not be reproduced or used in any manner whatsoever without the express written permission of the publisher except for the use of brief quotations in a book review or scholarly journal.

First Printing: 2019

ISBN: 978-1-7335565-1-4

Unless otherwise indicated, all Scripture quotations are taken from the Holy Bible, New Living Translation, copyright © 1996, 2004, 2007, 2013, 2015 by Tyndale House Foundation. Used by permission of Tyndale House Publishers, Inc., Carol Stream, Illinois 60188. All rights reserved. Scriptures marked KJV are taken from the King James Version (KJV): King James Version, public domain. Scriptures marked NIV are taken from the New International Version (NIV): Scripture was taken from The Holy Bible, New International Version ®. Copyright© 1973, 1978, 1984, 2011 by Biblical, Inc.™. Used by permission of Zondervan. Scriptures marked ESV are taken from The Holy Bible, English Standard Version® (ESV®) Copyright © 2001 by Crossway, a publishing ministry of Good News Publishers. All rights reserved. ESV Text Edition: 2016. Scripture quotations taken from the Amplified® Bible (AMP), Copyright © 2015 by The Lockman Foundation. Used by permission. www.Lockman.org

---

Glorious Works Publishing
201 Bywood Ave. #2214
Upper Darby, PA 19082
www.gloriousworkspublishing.com

Special discounts are available on bulk purchases or by corporations, associations, educators, and others. For details, contact publisher at admin@gloriousworkspublishing.com.

Glorious Works Publishing can bring authors to your live events. For more information or to book an event, contact Glorious Works Publishing at admin@gloriousworkspublishing.com or visit our website at www.gloriousworkspublishing.com.

Dedication

To every woman who has wondered what, specifically, she was created for;

To every woman who has yearned for more meaning in her life;

To every woman who has wanted to experience true success and fulfillment;

To every woman who is pursuing purpose;

I dedicate this book to you.

Acknowledgments

Thank You, God, for creating me with purpose and allowing me to identify and pursue it. Thank You, for using me to touch the lives of many, some of whom I will never meet, by creating this resource. My prayer is that in everything that I do, that Your Will be done and that You be glorified.

Thank you to my children, Cameron and Sabrina, who challenged me and encouraged me to complete this project. It is an honor to be your mother. My prayer is that my example of pursuing God and pursuing purpose would drive you to seek after God and His unique purpose for your lives.

Thank you to my exclusive book launch team. Thank you for partnering with me and the vision that God gave to me. My prayer is that your participation in promoting this book will ignite a stronger desire in you to pursue your purpose in life.

Thank you to Glorious Works Publishing. May this work, that God entrusted to me, bring glory back to Him. I pray that each work that you publish brings glory to God.

Thank you to everyone who supported me and everyone who will pick this book up with or without the desire and intention to pursue purpose. I pray that these words will reach you where you are and transform your life forever.

Table of Contents

Introduction 11

Key 1:

Discover Purpose in Your Past and Pain 13

Key 1.1 What was my family life like growing up?

Key 1.2 What did my relationships with my peers and authority figures look like?

Key 1.3 What events in my life are most memorable and why?

Key 1.4 Who inspired me or who have I admired and why?

Key 1.5 What questions did I have growing up that I never asked or were never answered?

Key 1.6 Who do I need to forgive (myself included) or who do I need to ask for forgiveness?

Key 1.7 How can I apply what I have learned about my past to positively change my present and future?

Key 1.8 What traumatic or painful experiences have I left unresolved and why have I not sought healing or resolution?

Key 1.9 What characteristics do I possess that allow me to overcome my traumatic or painful experiences and who can I confide in or reach out to for support in resolving my traumatic or painful experiences?

Key 1.10 How can I help prevent others from experiencing similar painful experiences as myself or help those who have already experienced similar painful experiences?

Key 2:

Discover Purpose in Your

Position and Posture 63

Key 2.1 What are my expectations for the life stage that I am in right now and how does my reality compare with my expectations?

Key 2.2 Where did I acquire my expectations for the life stage that I am in right now?

Key 2.3 Why am I working at the company that I am currently working at?

Key 2.4 Why do I live where I am currently living?

Key 2.5 How can I intentionally, positively impact and be impacted by the people who I frequently encounter?

Key 2.6 How do I respond to unfulfilled expectations?

Key 2.7 What is my approach to dealing with seemingly difficult people or ideas that differ from my own?

Key 2.8 How would those closest to me describe my general outlook on life?

Key 2.9 How can I allow my attitude, decisions, and reactions to better reflect the impression that I would like to leave with others?

Key 3:

Discover Purpose in Your

Personality and Passion 99

Key 3.1 What have I discovered about myself that may come as a surprise to some (including myself)?

Key 3.2 What areas of my personality would I change, if I could?

Key 3.3 How can I intentionally put forth the time and effort to get to know myself?

Key 3.4 What do I find myself talking about most often?

Key 3.5 What problems or issues deeply upset me?

Key 3.6 What would I spend the majority of my time doing, if money was not an option?

Key 3.7 What areas of helping others bring me the most joy?

Key 3.8 How can I become a solution to a problem that I'm passionate about?

Key 4: Discover Purpose in Your Potential and Payment 133

Key 4.1 What comes naturally for me?

Key 4.2 What motivates me?

Key 4.3 What is the biggest hindrance that can prevent me from reaching my fullest potential?

Key 4.4 How can I utilize my natural talents, strengths, and motivators to realize the possibilities in my life?

Key 4.5 What specific costs of my time, energy and resources have I paid to achieve my goals and fulfill my purpose in life and how much am I willing to pay?

Key 4.6 What am I willing to sacrifice in order to achieve my goals?

Key 4.7 What is the timeframe that I expect to see a return on my investments of time, energy and resources for my goals and my purpose in life; and how would I respond if I did not receive a return on my investments of time, energy and resources for my goals and my purpose in life?

Key 5: Pursue Your Purpose 161

Key 5.1 Reflect

Key 5.2 List

Key 5.3 Share

Key 5.4 Do

Key 5.5 Check

Key 5.6 Repeat

About the Author 207

INTRODUCTION

Welcome to the Pursuing Purpose Workbook: 5 Keys to Fulfilling Your God-Given Purpose. The Pursuing Purpose Workbook is designed to propel women into discovering and fulfilling their purposes in every area of their lives. It will help you identify the purpose of your past, position, and passion among other key identifiers. You will answer questions such as: How can I apply what I have learned about my past to positively change my future? How does my reality compare with my expectations for the life stage that I am in right now? How can I become a solution to a problem that I'm passionate about? How much am I willing to pay of my time, energy and resources to achieve my goals and fulfill my purpose in life?

Pursuing Purpose will also give you practical next steps to take to assist you in seeing the manifestation of your goals, dreams and purpose. It is thought provoking and action inspiring. Whether you are a college student trying to figure out what your next steps are or you are well established in your life and career, but sense that there is more in life waiting for you, Pursuing Purpose is the bridge to help get you from where you are to where you need to be—living a purposeful life.

As you work through this workbook, take your time to digest, reflect and respond to the questions that are designed to probe your heart and mind. Provide, analyze and assess your responses. The more transparent and authentic that you are with yourself as you work your way through this workbook, the more beneficial it will be to you. Also, take advantage of my accompanying book, Pursuing Purpose: 5 Keys to Fulfilling Your God-Given Purpose. In the book, I share examples of my highs, lows, strengths and weaknesses, reflections and discoveries that projected me into living out my purpose. My experiences and responses are simply a guide for you. This workbook puts the focus on you and is designed to give you ample space to record and reflect on your responses and reinforce and elaborate on key concepts and ideas through worksheets, visuals, schedules, checklists and other resources.

Often, when we hear the idea of finding purpose in our lives, we think singularly, as if there is only one thing that we can or should do in life. The reality is that our purpose in life is to identify what we were created to do and do it in every area of our lives. This workbook will not only help you to pursue your purpose, but also uncover the hidden purposes in your life. As long as you are living, continue pursuing purpose.

<3 always,
Your sister in Christ,
Kyra Lanae

KEY 1:

DISCOVER PURPOSE IN YOUR PAST AND PAIN

past | noun

1. the time or a period of time before the moment of speaking or writing

pain | noun

1. physical suffering or discomfort caused by illness or injury or mental suffering or distress

Key 1.1 What was my family life like growing up?

Did you grow up as an only child or were you in a long line of siblings? Were you raised by your parents, grandparents or maybe foster or adoptive parents? Did you have a close-knit extended family or did you grow up only knowing a few family members? What was the atmosphere like in your home? Was it warm, loving and comforting or was it cold and filled with despair?

As you walk down memory lane, deeply think about the mechanics and nuances of your family life. Discovering your past requires you to recall it and begin to dissect it. Subtle things that we overlooked growing up have significance in our lives. Both the unnoticed and profound details help shape who we are and how we perceive and function in our lives several years later.

Whatever the circumstances we found our family life, whether they were favorable or disheartening, they were significant and affected us into adulthood. Dissecting some of those circumstances can help decode the reasoning behind our choices and behaviors.

Now, you answer: What was my family life like growing up?
_____
_____
_____
_____
_____
_____
_____
_____
_____
_____

The past is never where you think you left it.

Katherine Anne Porter

The role that faith played within my family was
_____
_____
_____

What I liked about my family was
_____
_____
_____

What I thought was strange about my family was
_____
_____
_____

What I wanted to replicate that I gleaned from my family was
_____
_____
_____

What I stayed away from that I witnessed or experienced within my family was
_____
_____
_____

Color in the graph for each stage showing how satisfied or dissatisfied you were with your family life.

Childhood

- Very Satisfied
- Satisfied
- Neutral
- Dissatisfied
- Very Dissatisfied

Adolescence

- Very Satisfied
- Satisfied
- Neutral
- Dissatisfied
- Very Dissatisfied

Young Adulthood

- Very Satisfied
- Satisfied
- Neutral
- Dissatisfied
- Very Dissatisfied

Key 1.2 What did my relationships with my peers and authority figures look like?

Think back to your middle and high school years. Think about the awkward stages of puberty, peer pressure and transitioning into adulthood. Those years are critical. Were you the one who was sure of who you were and rose above the pressures of teenage years or were you susceptible to the common challenges of trying to be who your friends wanted you to be? Were you bullied or were you a bully or were you neither?

Often, how we react or interact with others is indicative of how we have acted in the past or how we would have preferred to behave in the past. If you had healthy relationships, it is easier for you to replicate those types of relationships. Conversely, if you did not have healthy relationships, your desire to give what you lacked could override your experiences.

Now, you answer: What did my relationships with my peers and authority figures look like?

_____
_____
_____
_____
_____
_____
_____
_____
_____
_____
_____
_____

Do not be misled: Bad company corrupts good character.

1 Corinthians 15:33 NIV

Who were the trusted adults that you could confide in?
_____

Did you seek help when you felt that you needed adult intervention? When?
_____
_____
_____

If you could go back to your adolescent years, what would you do differently?
_____
_____
_____

What areas of your life, during your adolescent years, did you handle admirably?
_____
_____
_____

What examples do you vividly remember being set for you by your authority figures during your adolescent years?
_____
_____
_____

> **Circle the character traits you possessed during your adolescent years. Underline the character traits that your closest group of friends possessed during your adolescent years. Place a check mark beside the character traits that the authority figures in your life possessed during your adolescent years.**

Agreeable	Passionate	Unreliable
Authentic	Self-disciplined	Dishonest
Clean	Responsible	Greedy
Compassionate	Respectful	Discouraging
Cooperative	Trustworthy	Inconsiderate
Kind	Unselfish	Foolish
Optimistic	Brave	Obnoxious
Curious	Forgiving	Unhealthy
Educated	Aggressive	Prejudice
Ethical	Argumentative	Anxious
Grateful	Bossy	Impatient
Hardworking	Cowardly	Lazy
Innocent	Dangerous	Neglectful
Inventive	Devious	Fearful
Organized	Disobedient	Forgetful
Exciting	Petty	Envious

Key 1.3 What events in my life are most memorable and why?

Reviewing the chapters in the stories of our lives, some stick out more prominently than others. There are memories that seem to be etched in our hearts forever while others fade away. The ups and downs of life cause some of them to bring back fond memories while others are recollections of unspeakable horror.

Whether wonderful or miserable, we hold on to the memories that we hold on to for a reason. Whether we are conscious of it or subconsciously, those memories affect our worlds. The choices we make, the way that we respond and even some of the beliefs that we hold on to so tightly are tied to our memories.

Now, you answer: What events in my life are most memorable and why?
_____
_____
_____
_____
_____
_____
_____
_____
_____
_____

List the positive memories in your life:

Amusing

Loving

Admirable

Exciting

Courageous

Adventurous

List the negative memories in your life:

Hostile

Disrespectful

Critical

Insulting

Inconsiderate

Disappointing

Think Space

This is your space to think, elaborate on a topic, if needed, and write or draw.

Think Space

This is your space to think, elaborate on a topic, if needed, and write or draw.

Key 1.4 Who inspired me or who have I admired and why?

Who we admire reveals plenty about how we perceive ourselves. Usually, we feel both a level of connection and dissociation with the people we admire. We see a commonality that links us to the person, but at the same time, we see something in them that shows that they have something or are doing something that we are not, or, in some cases, cannot have or do. Being inspired by someone or admiring someone is a balancing act. The key is to acknowledge, commend and draw from their strengths without becoming obsessive or envious.

The things we admire in others are the very things that we desire to be pulled out of us or highlighted in us. A part of us knows, deep down within, that it is possible. Witnessing it in others inspires us to discover it in our own lives.

Now, you answer: Who inspired me or who have I admired and why?

_____
_____
_____
_____
_____
_____
_____
_____
_____
_____
_____
_____

Blessed is he who has learned to admire but not envy, to follow but not imitate, to praise but not flatter, and to lead but not manipulate.

William Arthur Ward

I admired_____

and our relationship was

_____
_____
_____
_____

I admired_____

and our relationship was

_____
_____
_____
_____

How were your actions or ideas influenced by those whom you admired?

_____
_____
_____
_____
_____
_____
_____
_____

Remember that people are imperfect. Were you able to see both the strengths and weaknesses in those whom you admired?

Indicate both the strengths and weaknesses that you observed.

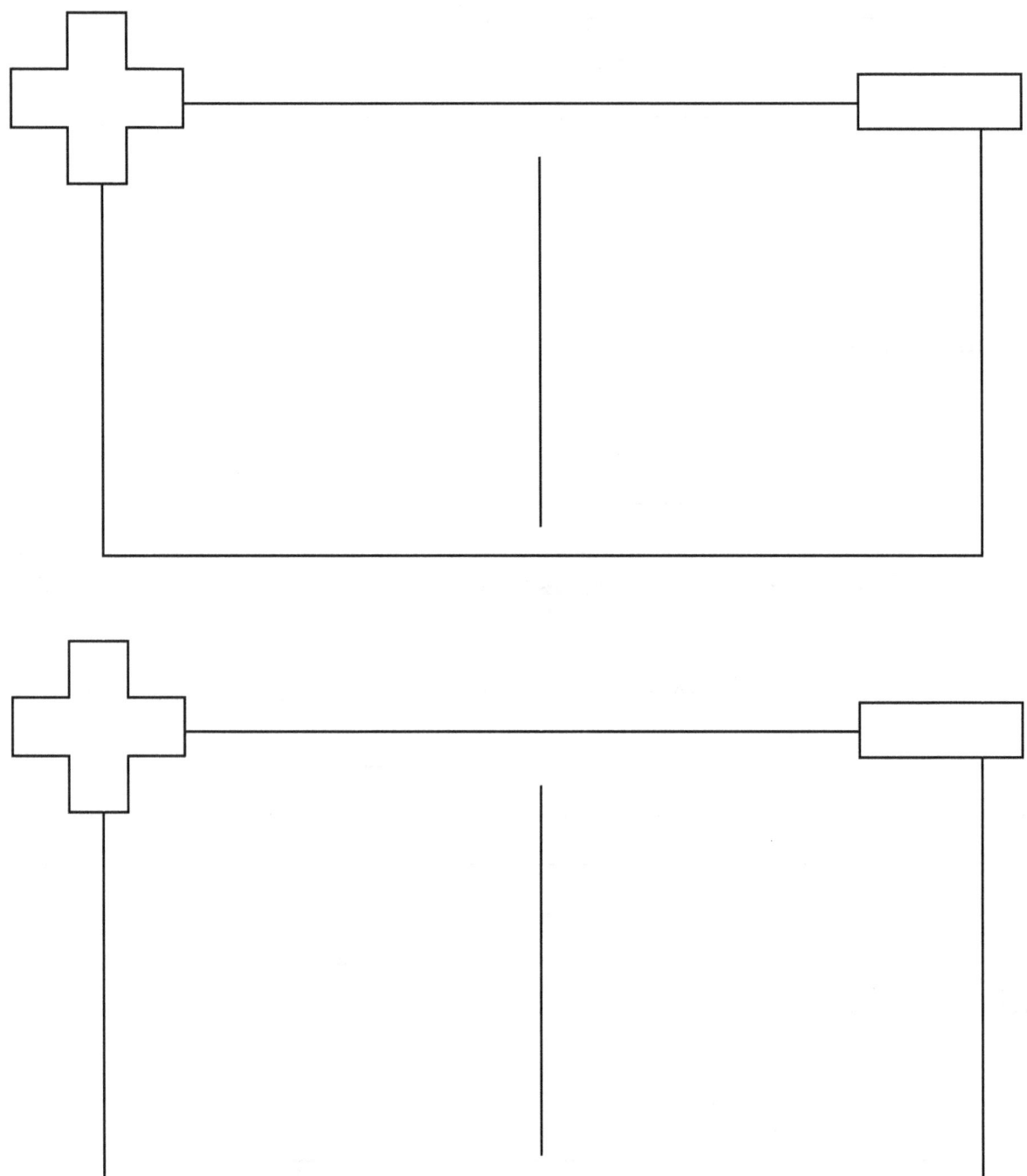

Key 1.5 What questions did I have growing up that I never asked or were never answered?

My mom grew up instilled with the notion that "children should be seen and not heard." The idea was that children did not have a voice. They were expected to be respectful, obedient and stay in a child's place. While I agree that children should be respectful, obedient and understand their position as a child, I also believe that children should be recognized as people. People, not only adults, have a desire to be seen, heard, acknowledged and valued. While children may not have the authority to act on every opinion that they have, it should be recognized that they do have an opinion. Even more so, they have questions. There are times when children can be erroneously viewed as disrespectful simply for desiring to gain a better understanding.

If there were ever any questions that you could not ask growing up, think about them and ask now. Ask and find an answer, if possible. If there are not any particular questions that you remember having that went unanswered, reflect on whether or not your voice was heard growing up. Were you free to gain an understanding of the world around you?

Now, you answer: What questions did I have growing up that I never asked or were never answered?

_____
_____
_____
_____
_____
_____
_____

He called a little child to him,
and placed the child
among them.
And he said:
'Truly I tell you,
unless you change
and become like little children,
you will never enter the kingdom
of heaven.'

Matthew 18:2-3 (NIV)

How did you know that your voice was heard as a child?

_____
_____
_____
_____

What made you feel valued as a child?

_____
_____
_____
_____
_____

How were you encouraged to express yourself as a child?

_____
_____
_____
_____

How did you feel most comfortable expressing yourself as a child?

_____
_____
_____
_____
_____

What places or with which groups of people were easiest and hardest to express yourself? Starting with 1, number from easiest to hardest.

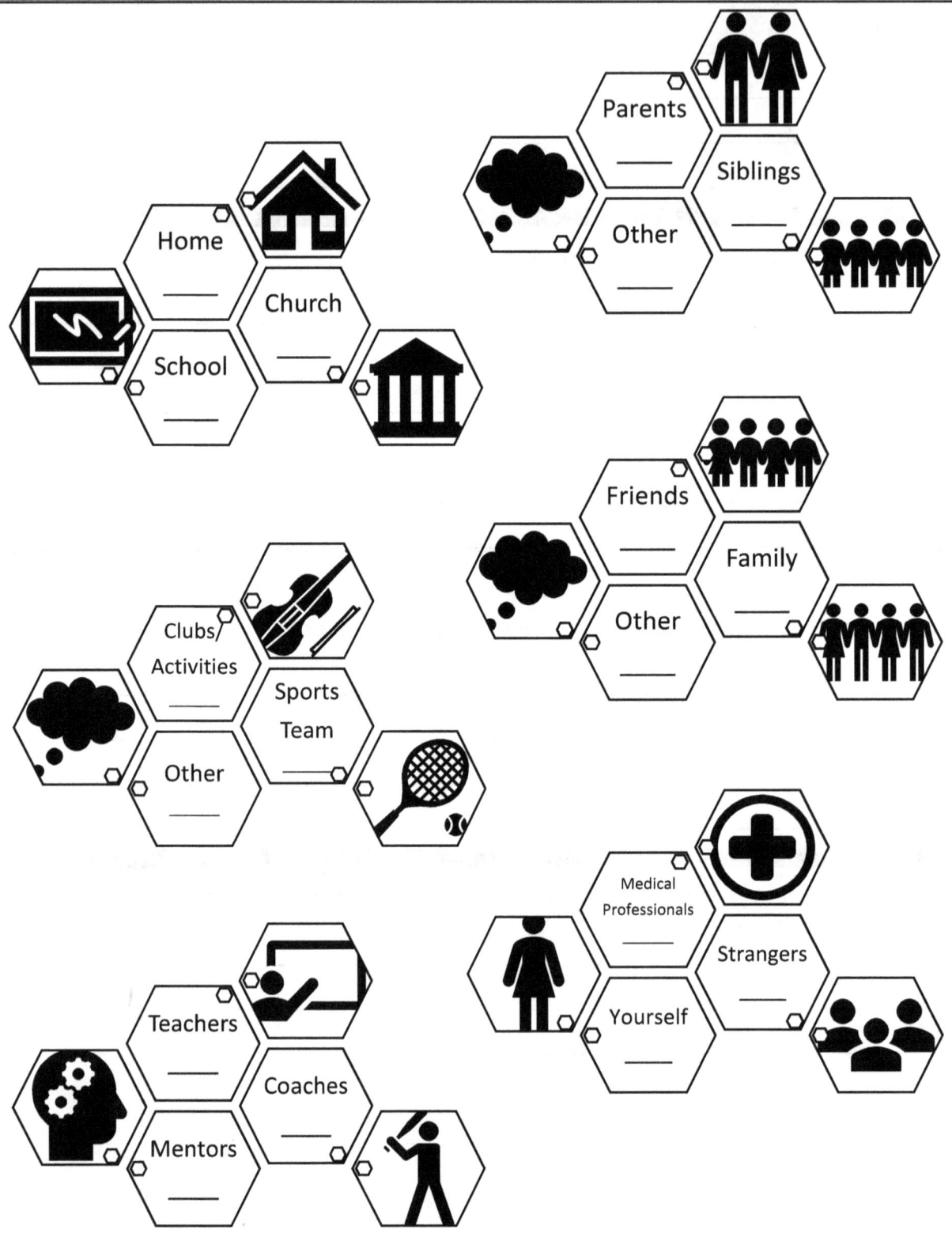

Think Space

This is your space to think, elaborate on a topic, if needed, and write or draw.

Think Space

This is your space to think, elaborate on a topic, if needed, and write or draw.

Key 1.6 Who do I need to forgive (myself included) or who do I need to ask for forgiveness?

Forgiveness can be a scary thing. The scary thing about forgiveness is that in order to forgive we have to acknowledge unfavorable experiences and mistakes that we might otherwise want buried and expunged from our memories. Forgiveness is humbling, powerful and freeing whether you are in the position to forgive or the position of asking for forgiveness.

When you forgive, you release whoever you are forgiving and that even includes yourself. Humility is required when you extend forgiveness because you admit that you were hurt by a person's actions. When you ask for forgiveness, you humble yourself and admit a fault. Whether or not the other person accepts your apology is between them and God. Your freedom comes in knowing that you acknowledged your mistake and attempted to correct it.

Now, you answer: Who do I need to forgive (myself included) or who do I need to ask for forgiveness?

_____
_____
_____
_____
_____
_____
_____
_____
_____

Then Peter came to him and asked, 'Lord, how often should I forgive someone who sins against me? Seven times?'

'No, not seven times,' Jesus replied, 'but seventy times seven!'

Matthew 18:21-22

I need to forgive_____

for_____

that happened_____.

I have been holding_____

captive for _____ days/weeks/months/years.

It is time to forgive_____.

I need to forgive_____

for_____

that happened_____.

I have been holding_____

captive for _____ days/weeks/months/years.

It is time to forgive_____.

I need to forgive_____

for_____

that happened_____.

I have been holding_____

captive for _____ days/weeks/months/years.

It is time to forgive_____.

> To be a Christian means to forgive the inexcusable because God has forgiven the inexcusable in you.
>
> C.S. Lewis

I need to forgive_____
for_____
that happened_____.
I have been holding_____
captive for _____ days/weeks/months/years.
It is time to forgive_____.

I need to forgive_____
for_____
that happened_____.
I have been holding_____
captive for _____ days/weeks/months/years.
It is time to forgive_____.

I need to forgive_____
for_____
that happened_____.
I have been holding_____
captive for _____ days/weeks/months/years.
It is time to forgive_____.

Key 1.7 How can I apply what I have learned about my past to positively change my present and future?

Our pasts have purpose, and our pasts affect our presents and futures whether we like it or not. Our pasts help shape who we are today and who we aspire to be tomorrow. Our pasts are something that we cannot ignore but rather acknowledge, accept and learn from. If we do not take the necessary steps in properly dealing with our pasts, then we are susceptible to holding on to it and even repeating its mistakes and errors in our presents and futures.

My mistakes were not in vain. They were learning experiences. My past was not in vain, and neither is yours.

Now, you answer: How can I apply what I have learned about my past to positively change my present and future?

_____
_____
_____
_____
_____
_____
_____
_____
_____
_____

Yesterday is history,

tomorrow is

a mystery,

today is a

gift of God,

which is why we call it

the present.

Bill Keane

Use the space to state what you have learned in the following areas:

Family Life

I learned

_____
_____
_____

and I can apply it to my life by

_____
_____
_____.

Memorable Events

I learned

_____
_____
_____

and I can apply it to my life by

_____
_____
_____.

Unanswered Questions

I learned

_____
_____
_____

I can apply it to my life by

_____
_____
_____.

Peers/Authority

I learned

_____
_____
_____

and I can apply it to my life by

_____
_____
_____.

People I admire

I learned

_____
_____
_____

and I can apply it to my life by

_____
_____
_____.

Forgiveness

I learned

_____
_____
_____

and I can apply it to my life by

_____
_____
_____.

Key 1.8 What traumatic or painful experiences have I left unresolved and why have I not sought healing or resolution?

It is sometimes comforting to tuck it away, to lock it in the closet or sweep it under the rug. The only caveat is that the rug begins to bulge. If you decide not to deal with your traumatic or painful experiences, eventually, in one way or another, they will deal with you. You may be able to stand in front of the closet door for ten, twenty or thirty or more years but at some point, the hinges will weaken, beginning to creak, and the very things that you tried so desperately to hold back in secrecy will burst out and become exposed. The Bible says, "For all that is secret will eventually be brought into the open, and everything that is concealed will be brought to light and made known to all" (Luke 8:17).

The most common reasons for concealing a traumatic or painful experience are shame, fear, and the torment of reliving the experience. The Word of God and godly counsel guides us in the healing process. Shame thrives in secrecy and fear lives in the unknown. 1 John 4:18 says, "There is no fear in love, but perfect love casts out fear. For fear has to do with punishment, and whoever fears has not been perfected in love." When we confront fear by embracing the love of God and the truth of His Word, we can move past our fears to receive the healing that we need. The beautiful thing about healing from a traumatic or painful experience is that it does not stop with you. Once you receive healing from a particular issue, it frees you up to extend healing to others involved in similar situations. That is what Paul was talking about in 2 Corinthians 1: 3-4, when he said, "Praise be to the God and Father of our Lord Jesus Christ, the Father of compassion and the God of all comfort, who comforts us in all our troubles, so that we can comfort those in any trouble with the comfort we ourselves receive from God."

As long as our trauma and pain are buried inside of us, it has the power to torment us on demand. When we expose the trauma and pain, we give ourselves the opportunity to heal. It is similar to a bandaged wound that is never permitted to breathe. There is comfort in covering up the wound, but it will never heal properly under those conditions.

Now, you answer: What traumatic or painful experiences have I left unresolved?

The LORD is close to the brokenhearted; he rescues those whose spirits are crushed.

Psalms 34:18

Evaluate each statement and mark "T" for true or "F" for false.

☐	I think about the event daily.
☐	I rarely think about the event.
☐	I often feel like I relive the experience.
☐	Thinking about the event keeps or wakes me up at night.
☐	I cry often when I think about the event.
☐	I get enraged when I think about the event.
☐	I feel scared when I think about the event.
☐	I feel empowered when I think about the event.
☐	I lost or gained a significant amount of weight following the event.
☐	I lost interest in things I enjoyed after the event.
☐	I feel like I became a better person since the event.
☐	I feel like I became a worse person since the event.
☐	I can talk openly about the event.
☐	I have not talked to anyone about the event.
☐	I feel like the event is resolved.
☐	I feel like the event is ongoing.
☐	I feel like the event is unresolved.

He heals the brokenhearted and bandages their wounds.

Psalms 147:3

Think Space

This is your space to think, elaborate on a topic, if needed, and write or draw.

Think Space

This is your space to think, elaborate on a topic, if needed, and write or draw.

> **Key 1.9 What characteristics do I possess that allow me to overcome my traumatic or painful experiences and who can I confide in or reach out to for support in resolving my traumatic or painful experiences?**

We were created in the image of God. That means that He has placed the characteristics that He has within us. God has equipped us to withstand the trauma and pain that life can bring by resting in Him and growing in our identity in Him. Because of the sacrifice of Jesus Christ, we have power and authority over the plans of the enemy and the traumatic and painful things that he brings into our lives to destruct us.

The best course of action is to prayerfully seek God's Will regarding your situation. The key is to reach out to someone. Do not keep the trauma and pain bottled up. There is no healing in hiding; only torment, fear and shame exist there.

Now, you answer: What characteristics do I possess that allow me to overcome my traumatic or painful experiences and who can I confide in or reach out to for support in resolving my traumatic or painful experiences?

_____
_____
_____
_____
_____
_____
_____

Turn your wounds into wisdom.

Oprah Winfrey

Color in the circles next to two characteristics from each group.

Next, fill them in the blanks.

- ○ Compassion
- ○ Peace
- ○ Confidence
- ○ Other:_____

- ○ Logic
- ○ Honesty
- ○ Desire to Help
- ○ Other:_____

- ○ Self-Discipline
- ○ Love
- ○ Commitment
- ○ Other:_____

- ○ Strength
- ○ Lack of Self-Pity
- ○ Forgiveness
- ○ Other:_____

- ○ Inner Drive
- ○ Hope
- ○ Courage
- ○ Other:_____

- ○ Faith
- ○ Focus
- ○ Resilience
- ○ Other:_____

I possess

_____, _____,
_____, _____,
_____, _____,
_____, _____,
_____, _____,
_____ and _____,
to help me overcome my traumatic or painful experiences.

Who can I confide in? Be sure to follow up and list the date when you reached out to a confidant.

Name:_____

Relation to me:_____

When will I reach out:_____

I reached out on:_____

Name:_____

Relation to me:_____

When will I reach out:_____

I reached out on:_____

Key 1.10 How can I help prevent others from experiencing similar painful experiences as myself or help those who have already experienced similar painful experiences?

We are not God, and we do not hold every situation in our hands, but we do have the ability to help prevent others from experiencing similar painful experiences that we have encountered. Even if we are not able to help prevent a situation, we can be available to help in the event that a situation does arise.

It is not our job to save people. Only Jesus can do that. However, we do have the ability to help prevent traumatic situations and support others after the fact.

Now, you answer: How can I help prevent others from experiencing similar painful experiences as myself or help those who have already experienced similar painful experiences?

_____
_____
_____
_____
_____
_____
_____
_____

He comforts us in all our troubles so that we can comfort others. When they are troubled, we will be able to give them the same comfort God has given us.

2 Corinthians 1:4

Who do I know who could be at risk of experiencing some of the traumatic or painful experiences that I have experienced? Be sure to follow up and list the date when you reached out to the people whom you listed.

Name:_____

Situation:
_____
_____
_____
_____

How can I help:
_____
_____
_____
_____

I reached out on:_____

Their Response:
_____
_____
_____
_____

Name:_____

Situation:
_____
_____
_____
_____

How can I help:
_____
_____
_____
_____

I reached out on:_____

Their Response
_____
_____
_____
_____

> Out of pain and problems come the sweetest songs and most gripping stories.
>
> Billy Graham

Who do I know who has experienced some of the traumatic or painful experiences that I have experienced?

Name:_____

Situation:
_____

How can I help:
_____
_____

I reached out on:_____

Their Response:
_____
_____

Name:_____

Situation:
_____

How can I help:
_____
_____

I reached out on:_____

Their Response:
_____
_____

Think Space

This is your space to think, elaborate on a topic, if needed, and write or draw.

Think Space

This is your space to think, elaborate on a topic, if needed, and write or draw.

KEY 2:

DISCOVER PURPOSE IN YOUR

POSITION AND POSTURE

po•si•tion | noun

1. a place where someone or something is located or has been put

pos•ture | noun

1. a particular way of dealing with or considering something; an approach or attitude

Key 2.1 What are my expectations for the life stage that I am in right now and how does my reality compare with my expectations?

As we go through life, we have expectations of what our lives should look like at various stages. While it is wise to have a plan and a sense of direction, we have to remember that we do not hold the master blueprint to our lives. Everything will not always pan out the way that we expect them to.

Proverbs 16:9 reminds us that, "We can make our plans, but the Lord determines our steps." Knowing this truth and holding on to it will help our realities match our expectations.

Now, you answer: What are my expectations for the life stage that I am in right now and how does my reality compare with my expectations?

_____
_____
_____
_____
_____
_____
_____
_____
_____
_____
_____

Many are the plans in the mind of a man, but it is the purpose of the Lord that will stand.

Proverbs 19:21

Compare your expectations (E) and reality (R) in the following areas:

- Spiritual (E)
- Spiritual (R)
- Family (E)
- Family (R)
- Health (E)
- Health (R)

- Romance (E)
- Romance (R)
- Finances (E)
- Finances (R)
- Business/Career (E)
- Business/Career (R)

- Personal Development (E)
- Personal Development (R)
- Social Life (E)
- Social Life (R)
- Recreation (E)
- Recreation (R)

Key 2.2 Where did I acquire my expectations for the life stage that I am in right now?

We live in a society that bombards us with messages, ideologies, and expectations that, if we are not careful, we can take on as our own. While our selfish desires can influence our expectations, the things and people around us can play a part in us acquiring expectations for our lives. James 4:1-3 speaks to both the desires in us and the focus that we place on what we see around us, in others.

What is causing the quarrels and fights among you? Don't they come from the evil desires at war within you? You want what you don't have, so you scheme and kill to get it. You are jealous of what others have, but you can't get it, so you fight and wage war to take it away from them. Yet you don't have what you want because you don't ask God for it. And even when you ask, you don't get it because your motives are all wrong— you want only what will give you pleasure. (James 4:1-3)

We have to be aware of where we acquire our expectations for our lives. Go to the creator of life Himself.

Now, you answer: Where did I acquire my expectations for the life stage that I am in right now?

_____
_____
_____
_____
_____
_____
_____
_____

Life is a journey that must be traveled no matter how bad the roads and accommodations.

Oliver Goldsmith

What do you feel each group listed is telling you about the direction in which you should take your life?

Family   Peers   Society

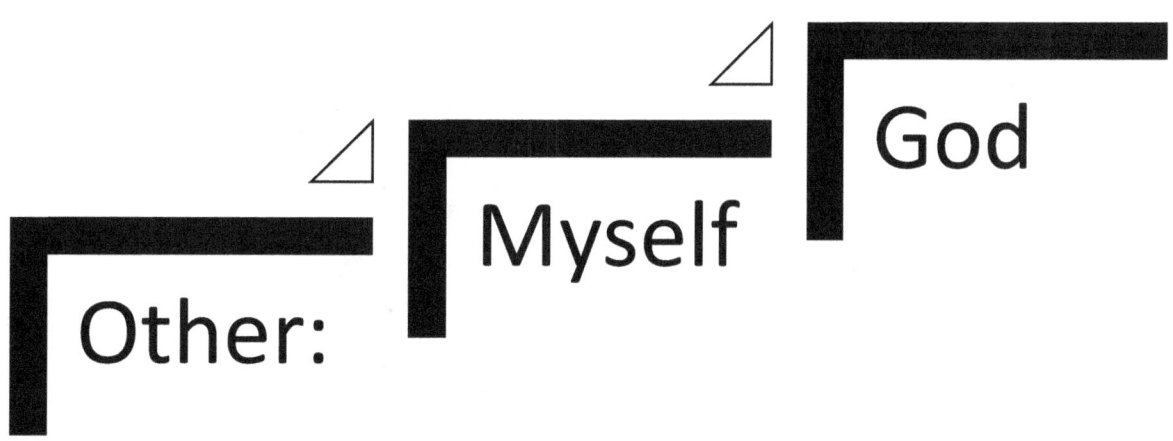

Other: Myself   God

Think Space

This is your space to think, elaborate on a topic, if needed, and write or draw.

Think Space
This is your space to think, elaborate on a topic, if needed, and write or draw.

Key 2.3 Why am I working at the company that I am currently working at?

The most obvious response to why we work where we do could be that we needed a job, and the company needed an employee and so the two came together and "Voilà!" However, the truth, although not so popular, is that you are working where you are because there is a specific reason why you should be there. In fact, the exact position you presently occupy was given to you for a purpose. God does not do anything by chance or mistake. He is purposeful in all that He does. That includes sending you to the company that you currently work for. Your paycheck and benefits are just a bonus. There is a purpose in the place where you are planted.

Now, you answer: Why am I working at the company that I am currently working at?

_____
_____
_____
_____
_____
_____
_____
_____
_____
_____
_____
_____

Work willingly at whatever you do, as though you were working for the Lord rather than for people.

Colossians 3:23

What do I get from and give to the company that I work at?

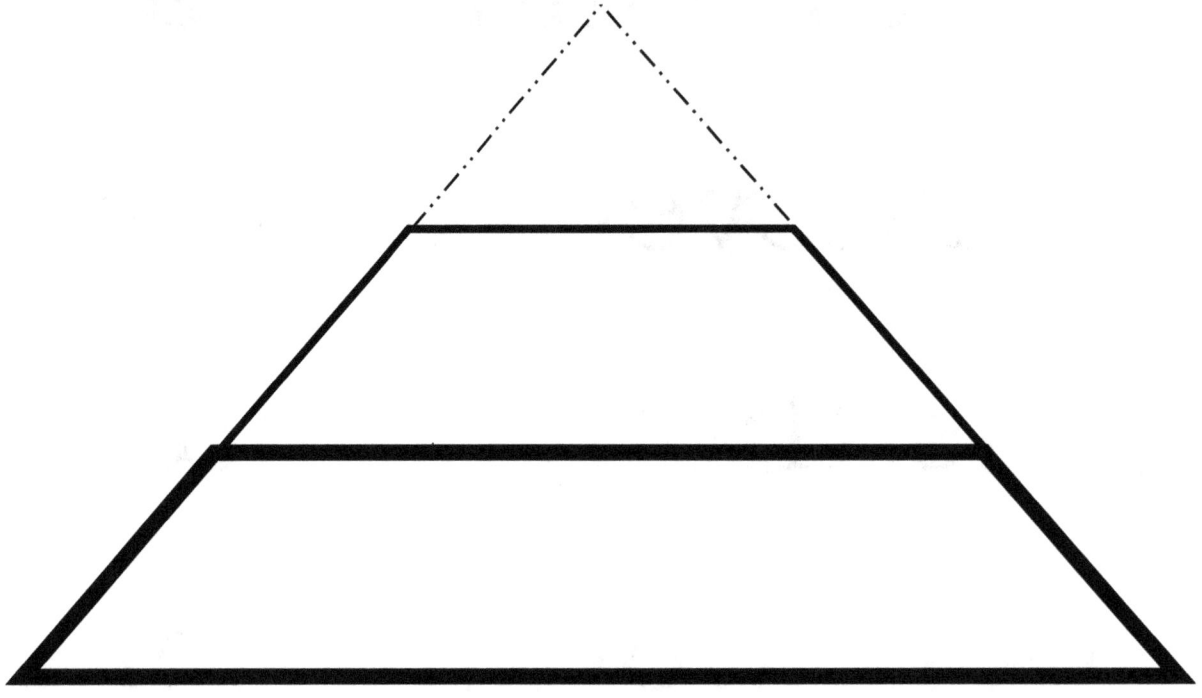

Get From

Give To

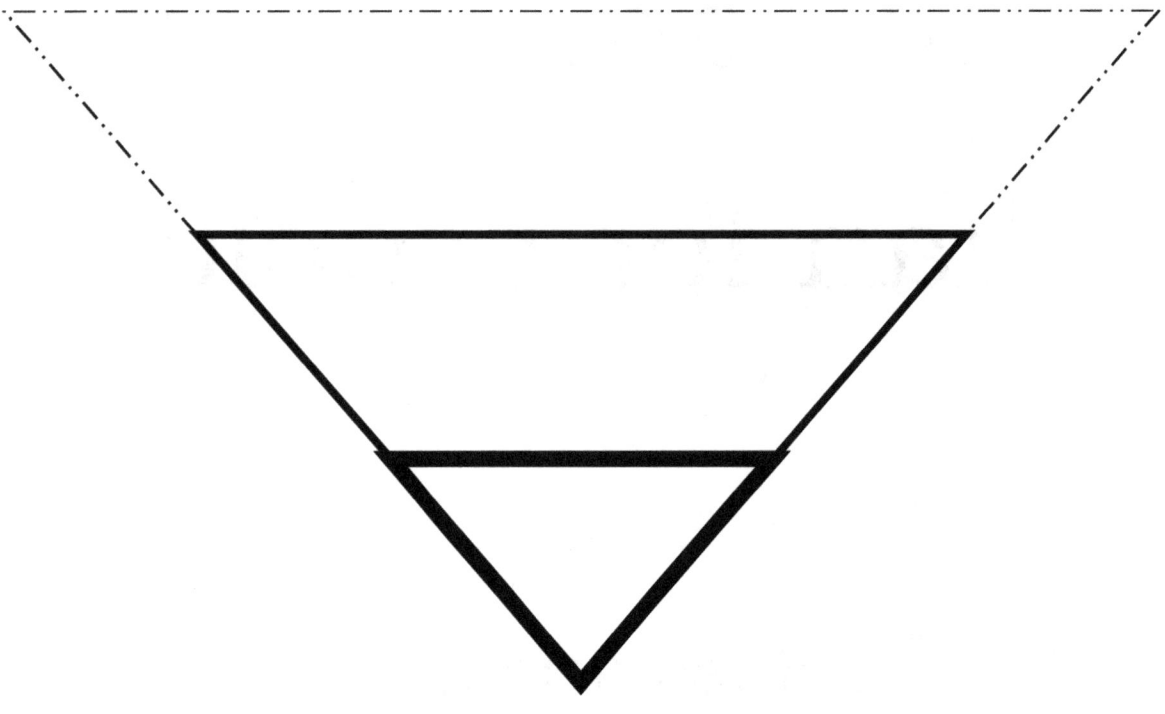

Key 2.4 Why do I live where I am currently living?

Where do you lay your head down at night? It may be in your dream home or maybe your starter home. Maybe the place that you call home is a temporary rental or even just a room in someone else's home. Wherever you currently are, there is a purpose for you being there. You may not even know the magnitude of your presence. The very thing that bothers you about where you are may possibly play an essential role in your purpose for being there.

What have you overlooked or complained about as it relates to where you live that God sees purpose in? It could be the neighborhood that you are desperately attempting to escape but inevitably find yourself. There are people in that place waiting for you to identify your purpose for being there.

Now, you answer: Why do I live where I am currently living?
_____
_____
_____
_____
_____
_____
_____
_____
_____
_____
_____
_____
_____

> "A city is more than a place in space, it is a drama in time."
>
> — Patrick Geddes

Answer the following questions:

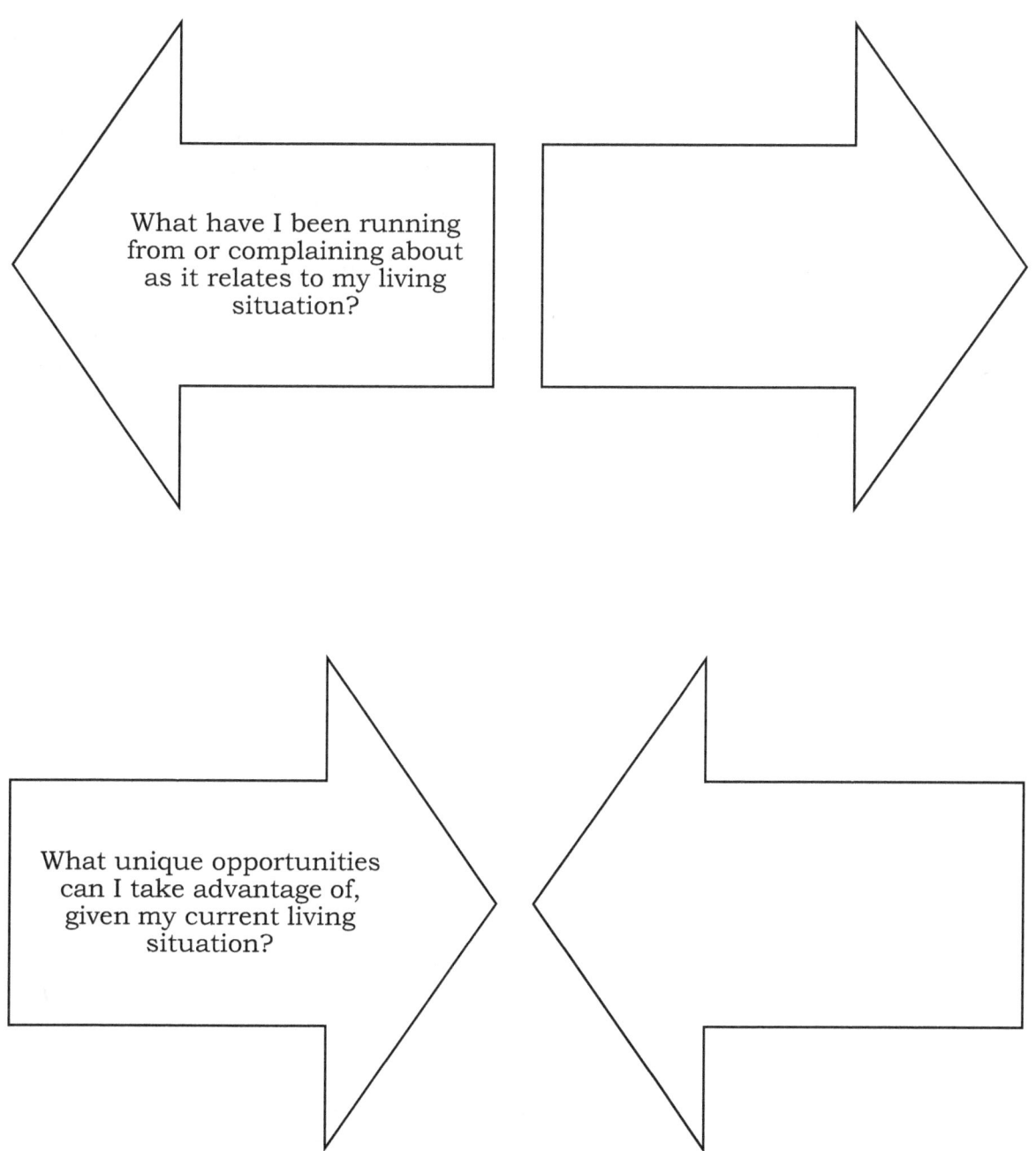

What have I been running from or complaining about as it relates to my living situation?

What unique opportunities can I take advantage of, given my current living situation?

Key 2.5 How can I intentionally, positively impact and be impacted by the people who I frequently encounter?

Can we agree on the fact that God is intentional? Every person that we encounter is there for a reason. Those whom we encounter frequently, whether at work, where we live, at church or even the grocery store are divinely connected to us. You might think that God would not be concerned about something as trivial as orchestrating every encounter that we have with someone, but might I remind you that Matthew 10:30 says that each hair on our heads has a number. Now, that is what I call caring about the tiniest details. So, now that we agree that those people are in our lives for a reason, what can we do about it? When we encounter people, it is for a purpose. They have the opportunity to impact us, and we have the opportunity to impact them.

Now, you answer: How can I intentionally, positively impact and be impacted by the people who I frequently encounter?

_____
_____
_____
_____
_____
_____
_____
_____
_____

Recognize that every interaction you have is an opportunity to make a positive impact on others.

Shep Hyken

Who can I intentionally impact? Be sure to follow up and list the date when you reached out to the people whom you listed.

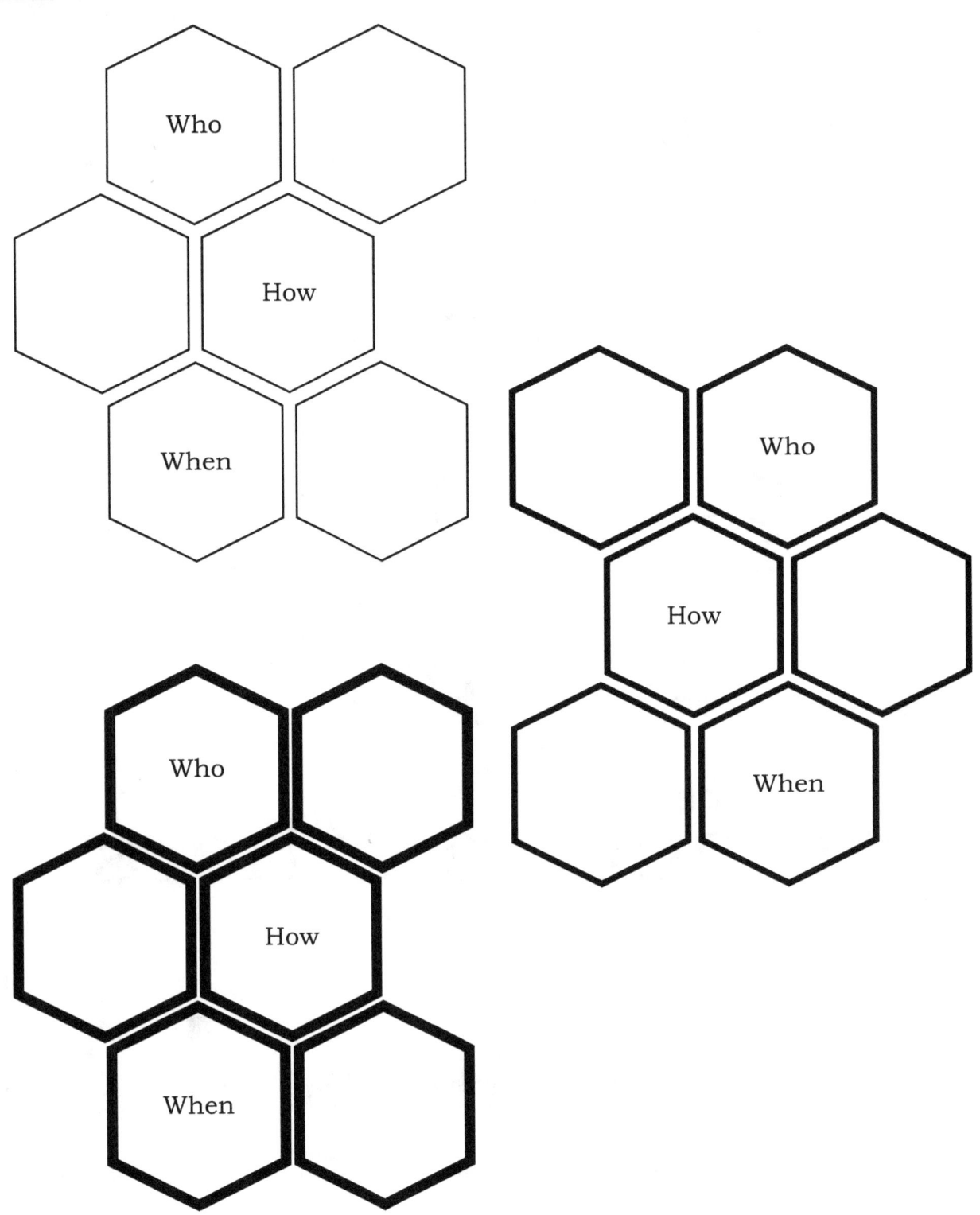

Think Space

This is your space to think, elaborate on a topic, if needed, and write or draw.

Think Space

This is your space to think, elaborate on a topic, if needed, and write or draw.

Key 2.6 How do I respond to unfulfilled expectations?

If you have lived for any amount of time, you can concur that things do not always go as planned. We learn that truth at a very young age. How we respond to unfulfilled expectations deals greatly with our perspective. If we think about when toddlers have unfulfilled expectations, in many cases, it results in a tantrum. At that age, their perspective is highly self-centered. Unfortunately, toddlers are not the only ones who can fall victim to a self-centered perspective. The truth is that our very nature is self-centeredness. That is why it is vital to renew our minds and take on God's perspective.

Romans 12:2 reminds us, "And do not be conformed to this world [any longer with its superficial values and customs], but be transformed *and* progressively changed [as you mature spiritually] by the renewing of your mind [focusing on godly values and ethical attitudes], so that you may prove [for yourselves] what the will of God is, that which is good and acceptable and perfect [in His plan and purpose for you]" (AMP). It takes time and effort to fill your mind with God's perspective so that when your expectations are unfulfilled, you do not respond with a tantrum.

When we have God's perspective, we can address disappointments with hope and joy. At times it may take some encouragement to remind yourself, but the key is to quickly remember. Remind yourself that God causes all things to work together for the good of those who love Him and are called according to His purpose. God is working out all of our unfulfilled expectations into a masterpiece, but we will never understand it or appreciate it if we continue to view it from our perspective.

Isaiah 55:8-9 reminds us that God's ways and thoughts are higher than our own. Do not become so fixated on your expectations that you miss out on what God is doing in your life.

Now, you answer: How do I respond to unfulfilled expectations?

_____

_____

It is the same with people as it is with riding a bike. Only when moving can one comfortably maintain one's balance.
Albert Einstein

> **Recount recent times when your expectations were unfulfilled.**
>
> **How did you respond?**

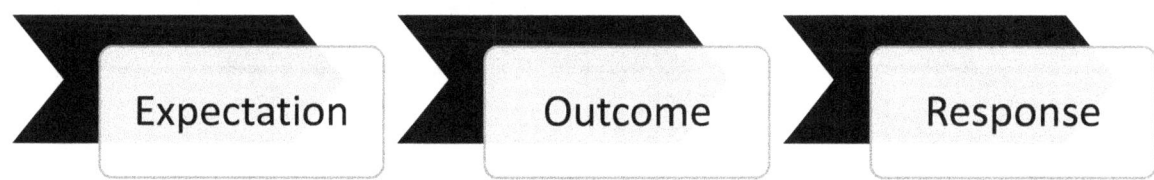

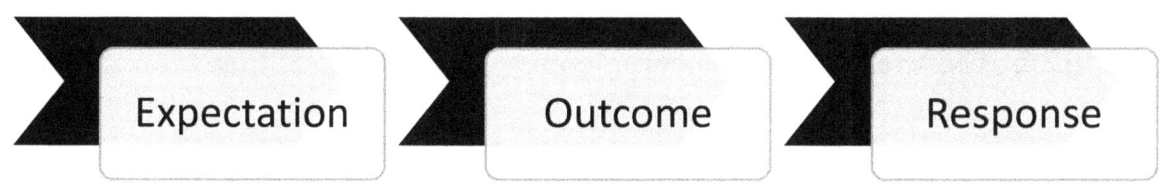

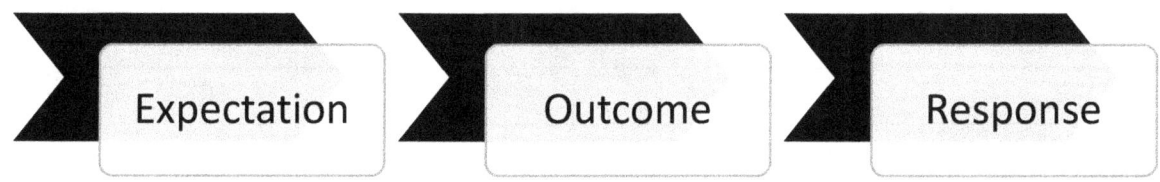

Key 2.7 What is my approach to dealing with seemingly difficult people or ideas that differ from my own?

In order to approach this question, think of the sandpaper people and ideas in your life. If you are wondering what sandpaper people or ideas are, they are the people or ideas that rub you the wrong way. How do you feel when you encounter them? Do you get frustrated or stressed out? Do you take it as an opportunity to evaluate your posture? Posture is a particular way of dealing with or considering something; it is an approach or attitude.

There is purpose in opposition. Seemingly difficult people can cause us to grow. Differing ideas are a necessary challenge. It does not feel good in that moment, but in the end, you become better. It is all about how you approach them.

Now, you answer: What is my approach to dealing with seemingly difficult people or ideas that differ from my own?

_____
_____
_____
_____
_____
_____
_____
_____
_____
_____

> Everything that irritates us about others can lead us to an understanding of ourselves.
>
> Carl Gustav Jung

Use the word bank to fill in the first blank in each group of words. Next, complete the statements with your responses.

Word Bank: Negative, Complaining, Aggressive, Stubborn, Oppressive, Bossy, Disrespectful, Lying, Gossiping, Lazy, Prideful

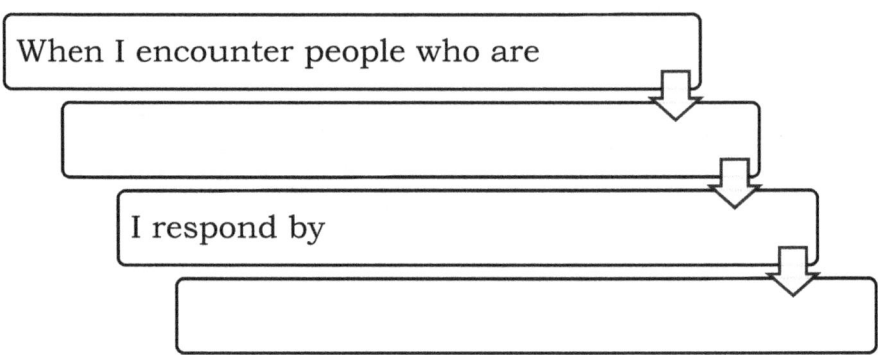

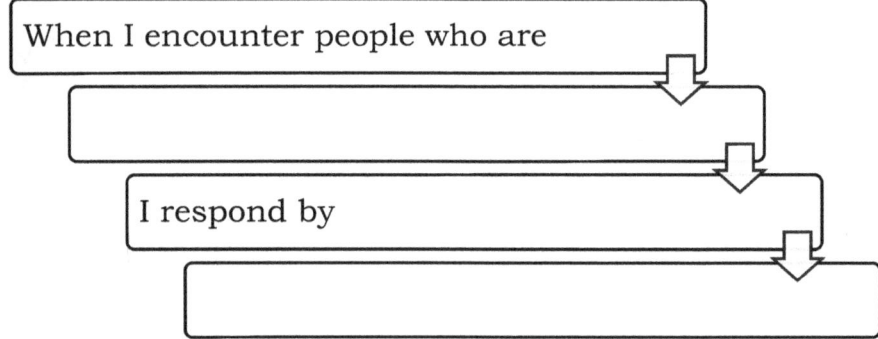

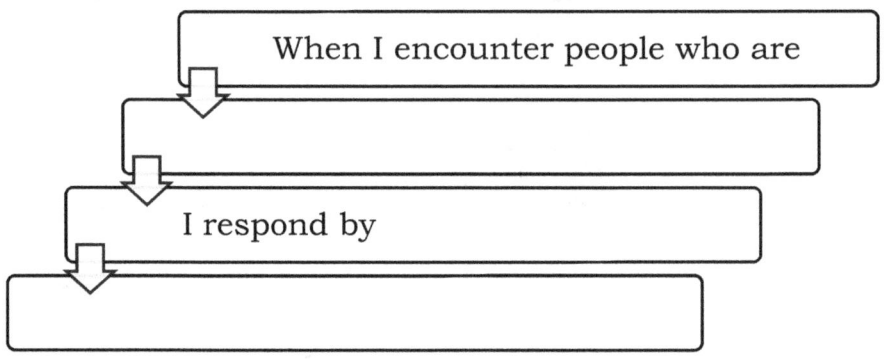

Use the word bank to fill in the first blank in each group of words. Next, complete the statements with your responses.

Word Bank: Religions, Politics, History, Sexuality, Culture, Economics, Women's Rights, Racism, Parenting

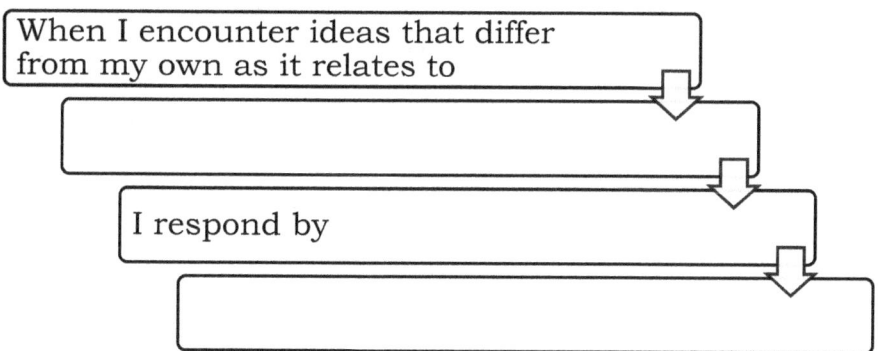

When I encounter ideas that differ from my own as it relates to _____

I respond by _____

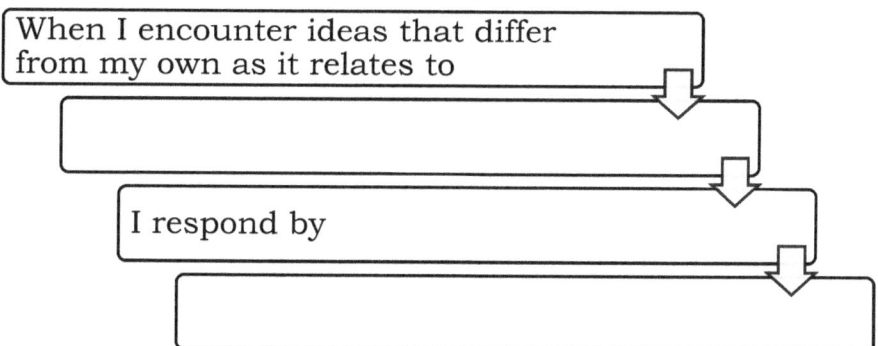

When I encounter ideas that differ from my own as it relates to _____

I respond by _____

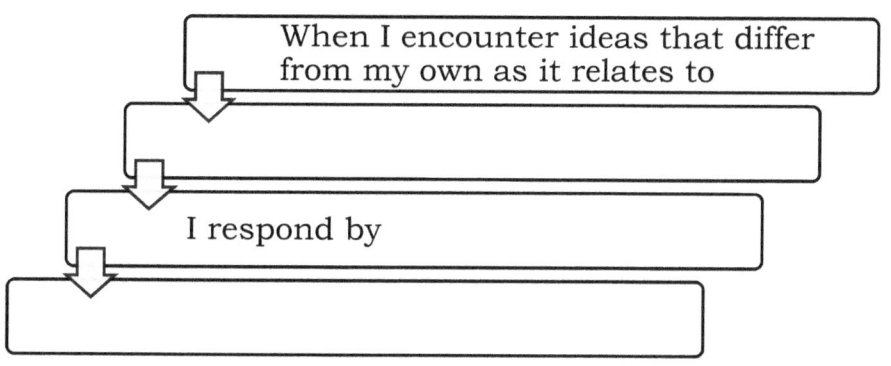

When I encounter ideas that differ from my own as it relates to _____

I respond by _____

Key 2.8 How would those closest to me describe my general outlook on life?

One of the benefits of having a community is that you have people around you that you can experience life with. Hopefully, there are a few people who are close enough to see the real you—not the social media, filters, perfect lighting, best angles, fake smiles, "I love life, and my life is great *all the time*"—you! So, if those closest to you were asked about you, what would they say? No one is perfect, and we all have areas to grow in, but would those closest to you describe your general outlook on life as positive or negative?

Personality aside, is your posture positive or negative? You do not have to smile nonstop or become a bubbly ball of cheer to look at life with joy. Joy is also described as great pleasure and enjoyment. Why would you want to turn that down?

Now, you answer: How would those closest to me describe my general outlook on life?
_____
_____
_____
_____
_____
_____
_____
_____
_____

> You make known to me the path of life; in your presence there is fullness of joy; at your right hand are pleasures forevermore.

Psalm 16:11

Evaluate each statement and mark "T" for true or "F" for false.

Those closest to me would say that I am optimistic. ☐

Those closest to me would say that I view the glass as half empty. ☐

Those closest to me would say that my reactions to unwanted circumstances are exaggerated. ☐

Those closest to me would say that they seek my help when they are dealing with challenges in life. ☐

Those closest to me would say that I make lemons out of lemonade. ☐

Those closest to me would say that they try to avoid me when I am dealing with challenges in life. ☐

Those closest to me would say that setbacks take a major toll on me. ☐

Those closest to me would say that I avoid risks. ☐

Those closest to me would say that they admire my poise during difficult circumstances. ☐

Those closest to me would say that I have an appropriate amount of faith in other people. ☐

Those closest to me would say that I handle victories with a balance of joy and humility. ☐

Those closest to me would say that I seek out learning opportunities when I make mistakes. ☐

Those closest to me would say that I had more good days than bad. ☐

Those closest to me would say that I embrace new things. ☐

Key 2.9 How can I allow my attitude, decisions, and reactions to better reflect the impression that I would like to leave with others?

Each day, we make choices. In fact, we make so many choices that we are not even conscious of some of the choices that we make. The key to allowing your attitude, decisions, and reactions to better reflect the impression that you would like to leave others with is to make conscious choices going in that direction. Of course, it is easier said than done, but it starts with a choice.

Making changes are typically not the easiest thing to do, but they always start with a choice and are followed up with action. It is not enough to say how you would like to see yourself in life. You have to follow through with the necessary actions to bring about that change.

Now, you answer: How can I allow my attitude, decisions, and reactions to better reflect the impression that I would like to leave with others?

_____
_____
_____
_____
_____
_____
_____
_____
_____
_____
_____

Life is 10% of what happens to you and 90% of how you react to it.

—Charles R. Swindoll

> **Circle the impressions that you think that you leave with others. Place a check mark next to impressions that you want to leave with others. Place an X next to impressions that you don't want to leave with others.**

I'm friendly.	I'm helpful.	I'm possessive.
I'm confident.	I'm generous.	I'm envious.
I'm trustworthy.	I'm clever.	I'm greedy.
I'm authentic.	I'm humble.	I'm prideful.
I'm capable.	I'm exciting.	I'm insincere.
I'm clean.	I'm respectful.	I'm irresponsible.
I'm compassionate.	I'm loyal.	I'm lazy.
I'm cooperative.	I'm patient.	I'm clumsy.
I'm optimistic.	I'm intelligent.	I'm critical.
I'm organized.	I'm perfect.	I'm deceitful.
I'm hardworking.	I'm aggressive.	I'm dishonest.
I'm honest.	I'm bossy.	I'm insulting.
I'm firm.	I'm argumentative.	I'm discouraging.
I'm ethical.	I'm dangerous.	I'm negative.
I'm brave.	I'm disobedient.	I'm shallow.
I'm strong.	I'm petty.	I'm sloppy.
I'm focused.	I'm disruptive.	I'm rude.
I'm gentle.	I'm unappreciative.	I'm ungrateful.
I'm creative.	I'm unreliable.	I'm sneaky.

What trends did you see when evaluating the impressions that you think you leave with others?

___

What trends did you see when evaluating the impressions that you would like to leave with others?

Think Space

This is your space to think, elaborate on a topic, if needed, and write or draw.

Think Space

This is your space to think, elaborate on a topic, if needed, and write or draw.

KEY 3:

DISCOVER PURPOSE IN YOUR PERSONALITY AND PASSION

---

per•son•al•i•ty | noun

1. the combination of characteristics or qualities

pas•sion | noun

1. an intense desire or enthusiasm for something

Key 3.1 What have I discovered about myself that may come as a surprise to some (including myself)?

How much time have you taken to get to know yourself? I mean *really* get to know yourself. Sometimes we go through life just going through the motions or following the crowd and not taking the necessary steps to actually get to know who we are or what we like. When you become intentional about discovering various parts of your personality, you will be able to be authentically you. The benefit of getting to know yourself more intimately is that you are able to apply who you are and how you are to situations around you. There are specific people and certain opportunities waiting for you to be uniquely you.

Now, you answer: What have I discovered about myself that may come as a surprise to some (including myself)?

_____
_____
_____
_____
_____
_____
_____
_____
_____
_____

> You made all the delicate, inner parts of my body and knit me together in my mother's womb. Thank you for making me so wonderfully complex! Your workmanship is marvelous—how well I know it.
>
> Psalms 139:13-14 NLT

> **Circle the activities that you have done. Place a question mark next to the activities that you would be interested in doing. Place a check mark next to the activities that you enjoyed. Place an X next to the activities that you didn't enjoy.**

Go to a concert

Go on a walk/run/hike

Pray

Cook a new recipe

Complete a DIY project

Go shopping

Stay in and watch a movie/favorite show

Clean your house

Go to a spa

Read a book

Go to the movies

Go to a nice restaurant

Paint

Go dancing

Start a blog

Get a manicure/pedicure

Travel

Rearrange your house/room

Complete brain teasers

Take a long, hot bath

Visit a museum

Go to the gym

Visit a library/bookstore

Browse photo albums

Read your Bible

Try a new workout class

Declutter/Organize

Find a new hobby

Go swimming

Complete a home improvement project

Sing karaoke

Bake a cake

Take a long drive

Explore nature

Turn off electronics

Volunteer

Hand write a letter to someone

Create a YouTube channel

Help a stranger

Take a free online class

Lay on a beach

Listen to a podcast

Get your finances in order

Make a time capsule

Learn to play a musical instrument

Write in your journal

Adopt a pet

What trends did you see when evaluating your experiences?

_____

_____

What trends did you see when evaluating your interests?

_____

_____

What trends did you see when evaluating your likes?

_____

_____

What trends did you see when evaluating your dislikes?

_____

_____

Key 3.2 What areas of my personality would I change, if I could?

Do not get this question twisted and begin to beat down the wonderful person you are. Evaluating areas that you would change about yourself should be reflective and inspiring. We all have areas that we can improve in and recognizing and being honest about them are the first steps to making any meaningful changes. Some things are hard-wired in us, but if it is an area that we would like to see growth, development or change, we can make adjustments to compensate for some of those personality traits.

God blessed you with a beautiful personality that is uniquely yours to serve his purpose for your life. You should keep and nurture this while working on correcting whatever flaws may exist in your character.

Now, you answer: What areas of my personality would I change, if I could?
_____
_____
_____
_____
_____
_____
_____
_____
_____
_____
_____
_____

> Don't try to take on a new personality; it doesn't work.
>
> Richard M. Nixon

Fill in the blanks.

I'm really good at _____
but I could be better at _____
and I could _____
to help change that.

I'm really strong in the _____
area, but could strengthen in the _____
area, and I could _____
to help change that.

I've mastered _____
but I still need to practice _____
and I could _____
to help change that.

I like my _____
but dislike my _____
and I could _____
to help change that.

Think Space

This is your space to think, elaborate on a topic, if needed, and write or draw.

Think Space

This is your space to think, elaborate on a topic, if needed, and write or draw.

Key 3.3 How can I intentionally put forth the time and effort to get to know myself?

You are an amazing person. The more you discover the many layers that you possess, the better you will be able to enjoy who you are and connect with those to whom you should be connected. Think about the last time you went on a date, not with a friend or significant other, but by yourself. Hanging out with those that you know and love or those who you would like to get to know and possibly love is great. There is definitely a time and space for that. Whether you are single or married, it is vital to continue to take yourself out (or stay in if you prefer) to spend time getting to know yourself better. As you grow and mature, your desires and perspectives change. That is one of the reasons that it should be a continual process of getting to know yourself.

Research the things that you are interested in and then, do them. See if it is something that looks good in theory but is not practically an interest of yours. You could go out and participate in every activity that comes to mind, but if you do not spend time reflecting on your experiences and preferences, you will miss out on the benefit of dating yourself.

Now, you answer: How can I intentionally put forth the time and effort to get to know myself?

_____
_____
_____
_____
_____
_____
_____
_____

> But the fruit of the Spirit is love, joy, peace, patience, kindness, goodness, faithfulness, gentleness, self-control; against such things there is no law.

Galatians 5:22-23

What can I do to get to know myself?

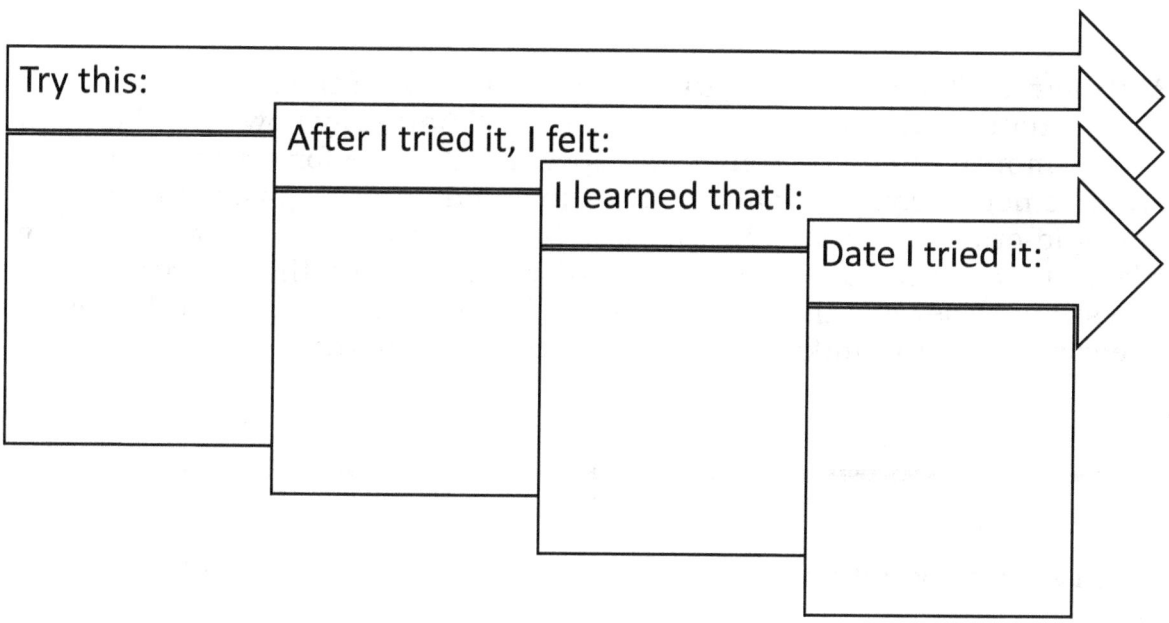

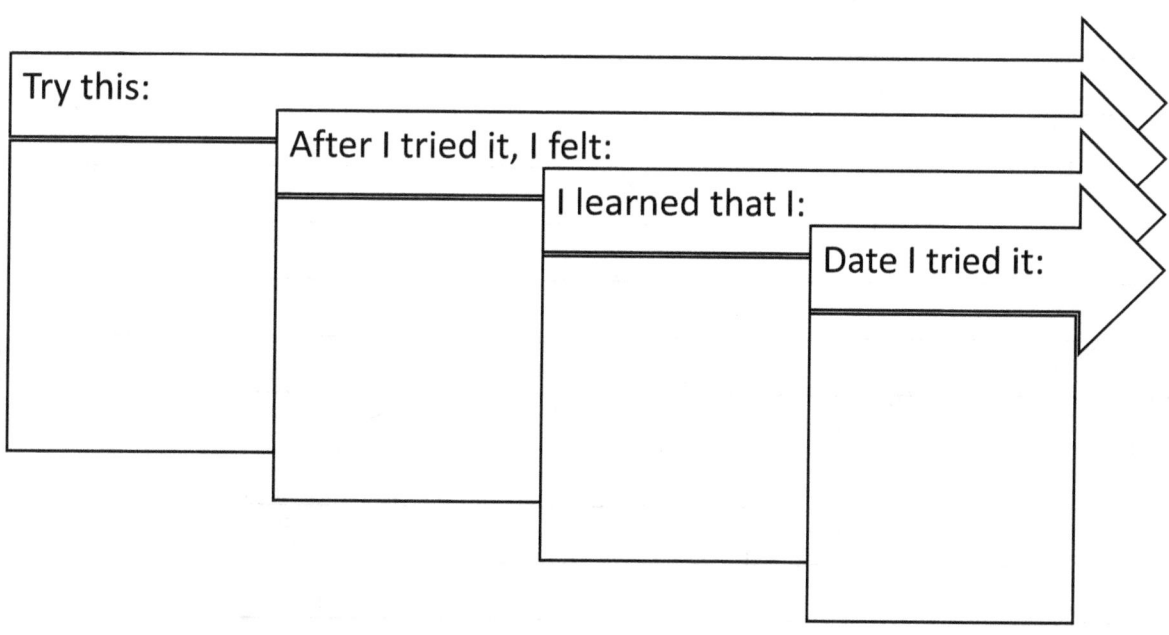

Key 3.4 What do I find myself talking about most often?

Matthew 12:34b says, "For out of the abundance of the heart the mouth speaks." Whatever you are passionate about will naturally flow out when you open your mouth. It can be something specific, like love for art or something general like negativity. Think about the things that you are passionate about. What would others say that your passion is based on what you say? Do they correlate? Our passions are clearly heard by the things that dominate our conversations. They say that actions speak louder than words but do not let that deceive you into thinking that our words are irrelevant.

Now, you answer: What do I find myself talking about most often?

> For where your treasure is, there your heart will be also.

Matthew 6:21

Time Tracker

Label the topics that you frequently talk about. Start at the center of the circle. Move towards the outer ring, shading in to indicate how much time you spend talking about those topics. The more time you spend, the closer your shaded area will be to the outer ring.

What are the top three things that you spend the majority of your time talking about? _____

How Much Time I Spend Talking About:

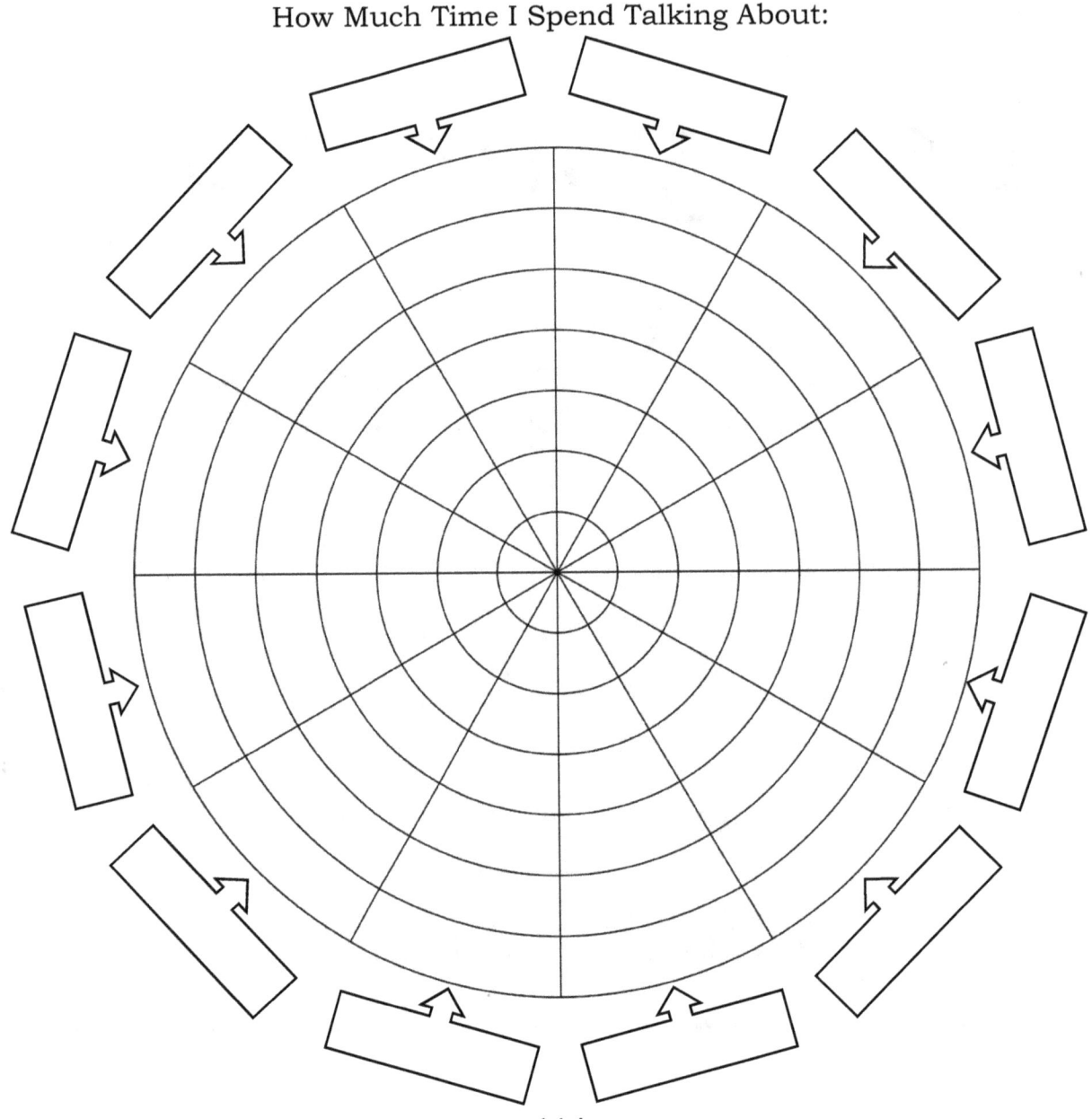

Key 3.5 What problems or issues deeply upset me?

We all have those things that extremely bother us that others may or may not notice or notice and do not care about. We are all unique and are not moved by the same issues. One person may have a burden for social injustice and another, homeless veterans. Almost all of us have a general sense of disdain or pity for problems that we see around us, but typically there is a problem or two that clinches us by the heart, grabs our attention and triggers our passion.

A problem or issue that deeply upsets us does not always have to be something that we have personally experienced. It could be something that we watched a loved one endure or even something that God has placed a burden in our heart for. More times than not, those problems are connected to us and demand our empathy.

Now, you answer: What problems or issues deeply upset me?
_____
_____
_____
_____
_____
_____
_____
_____
_____

> We may affirm absolutely that nothing great in the world has been accomplished without passion.
>
> Georg Wilhelm Friedrich Hegel

> **On a scale of 1-5, 1 being strongly disagree and 5 being strongly agree, rate the following statements.**

I have a strong desire to fight for women's rights. ☐

I have a strong desire to protect children. ☐

I have a strong desire to serve in politics. ☐

I have a strong desire to help the homeless. ☐

I have a strong desire to mentor women. ☐

I have a strong desire to serve in education. ☐

I have a strong desire to feed those in poor countries. ☐

I have a strong desire to share the Gospel. ☐

I have a strong desire to volunteer in my community. ☐

I have a strong desire to help pregnant women. ☐

I have a strong desire to serve in the medical field. ☐

I have a strong desire to speak in prisons. ☐

I have a strong desire to promote healthy living. ☐

I have a strong desire to make disciples of Jesus Christ. ☐

I have a strong desire to minimize human trafficking. ☐

I have a strong desire to serve in the military. ☐

I have a strong desire to counsel. ☐

I have a strong desire to care for the elderly. ☐

I have a strong desire to serve in law enforcement. ☐

Think Space

This is your space to think, elaborate on a topic, if needed, and write or draw.

Think Space

This is your space to think, elaborate on a topic, if needed, and write or draw.

Key 3.6 What would I spend the majority of my time doing, if money was not an option?

At some point or another, most of us have been asked a question similar to this. It could have been a high school essay topic, a team building activity at work or the prompting at a vision board party. The idea is that whatever we chose to do when money was not an option sheds light on our passion and true desires. One of the many barriers on the path to fulfillment is financial resource or ability. When that block is removed, the authenticity of what we really want and value are displayed.

Do not think for a moment that God placed massive dreams and passions in your heart to lie dormant. Begin to think of those things that you would spend the majority of your time doing if money was not an option as realistic things that you have the capacity to do, empowered by God.

Now, you answer: What would I spend the majority of my time doing, if money was not an option?

_____
_____
_____
_____
_____
_____
_____
_____
_____
_____

> What we spend our time on is probably the most important decision we make.
>
> Ray Kurzweil

Time Tracker

Start at the center of the circle and move towards the outer ring indicating how much time you spend on each area listed. Shade in the rings to allot the appropriate amount of time. As you allot more time in an area, your shaded area will move closer to the outer ring. Compare the three charts on the next three pages.

How Much Time I Spend On:

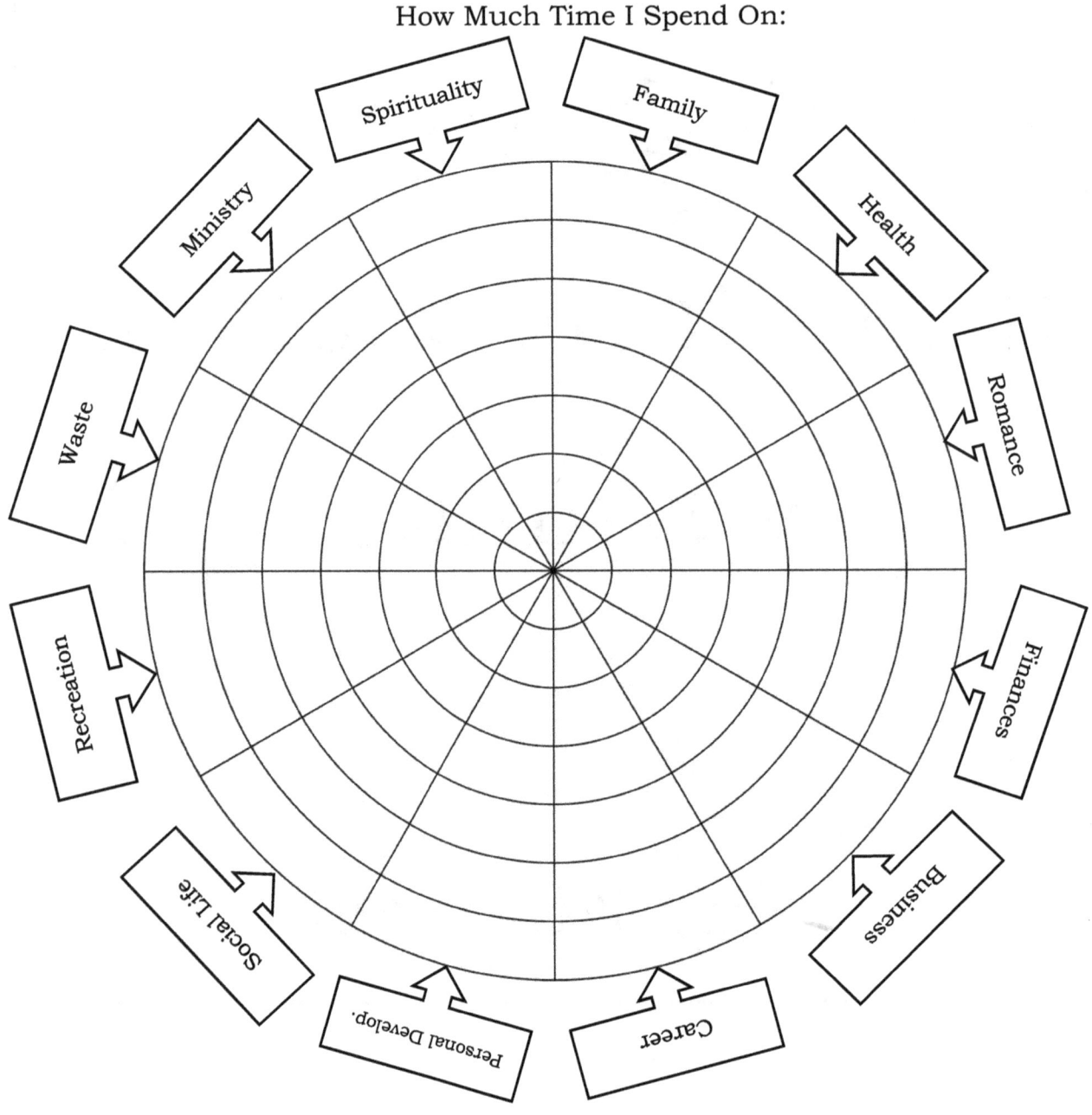

Time Tracker

Start at the center of the circle and move towards the outer ring indicating how much time you want to spend on each area listed. Shade in the rings to allot the appropriate amount of time. As you allot more time in an area, your shaded area will move closer to the outer ring.

How Much Time I Want to Spend on:

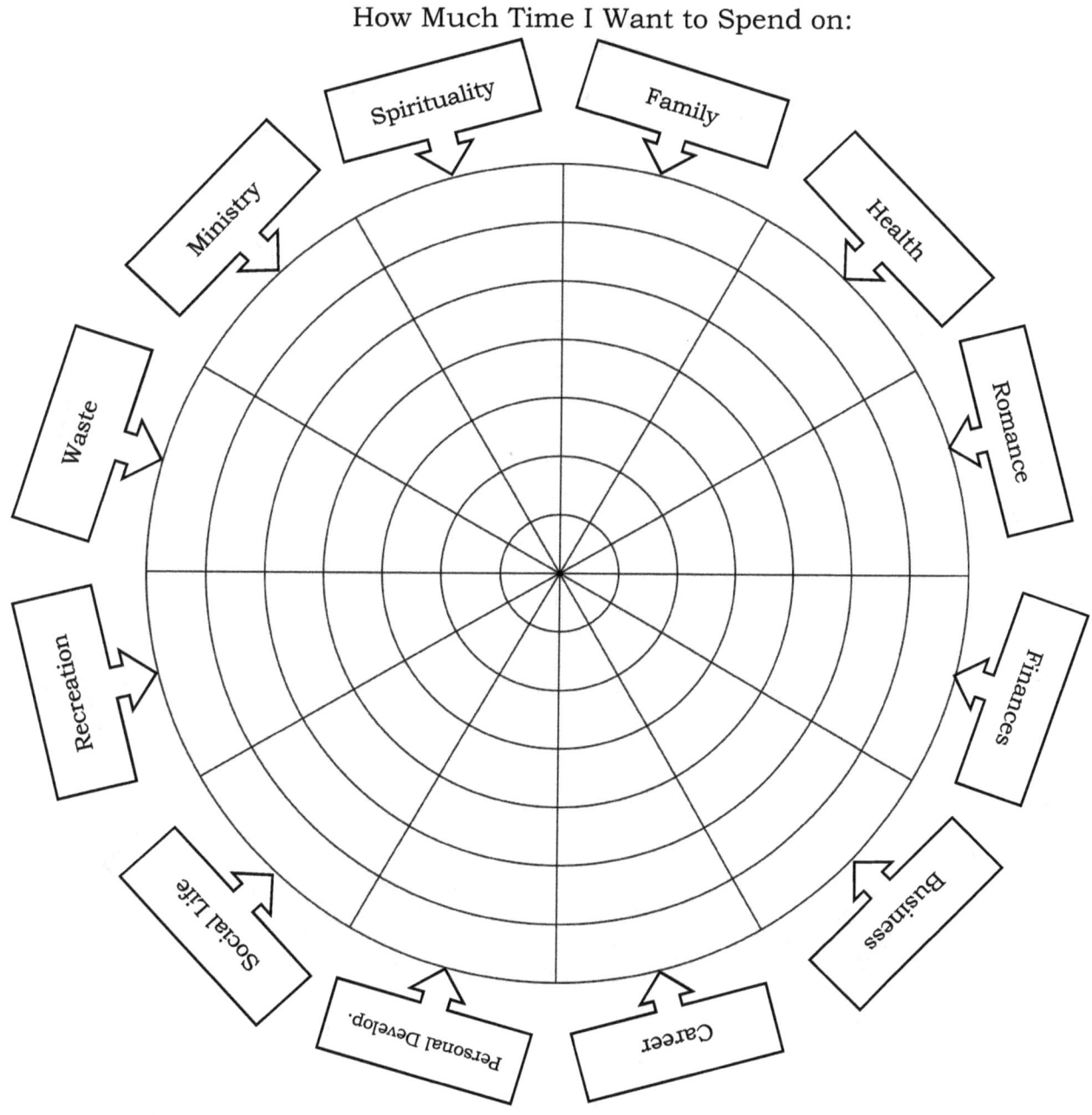

Time Tracker

Start at the center of the circle and move towards the outer ring indicating how much time you need to spend on each area listed. Shade in the rings to allot the appropriate amount of time. As you allot more time in an area, your shaded area will move closer to the outer ring. Compare the three charts on this page and the previous pages.

How Much Time I Need to Spend on:

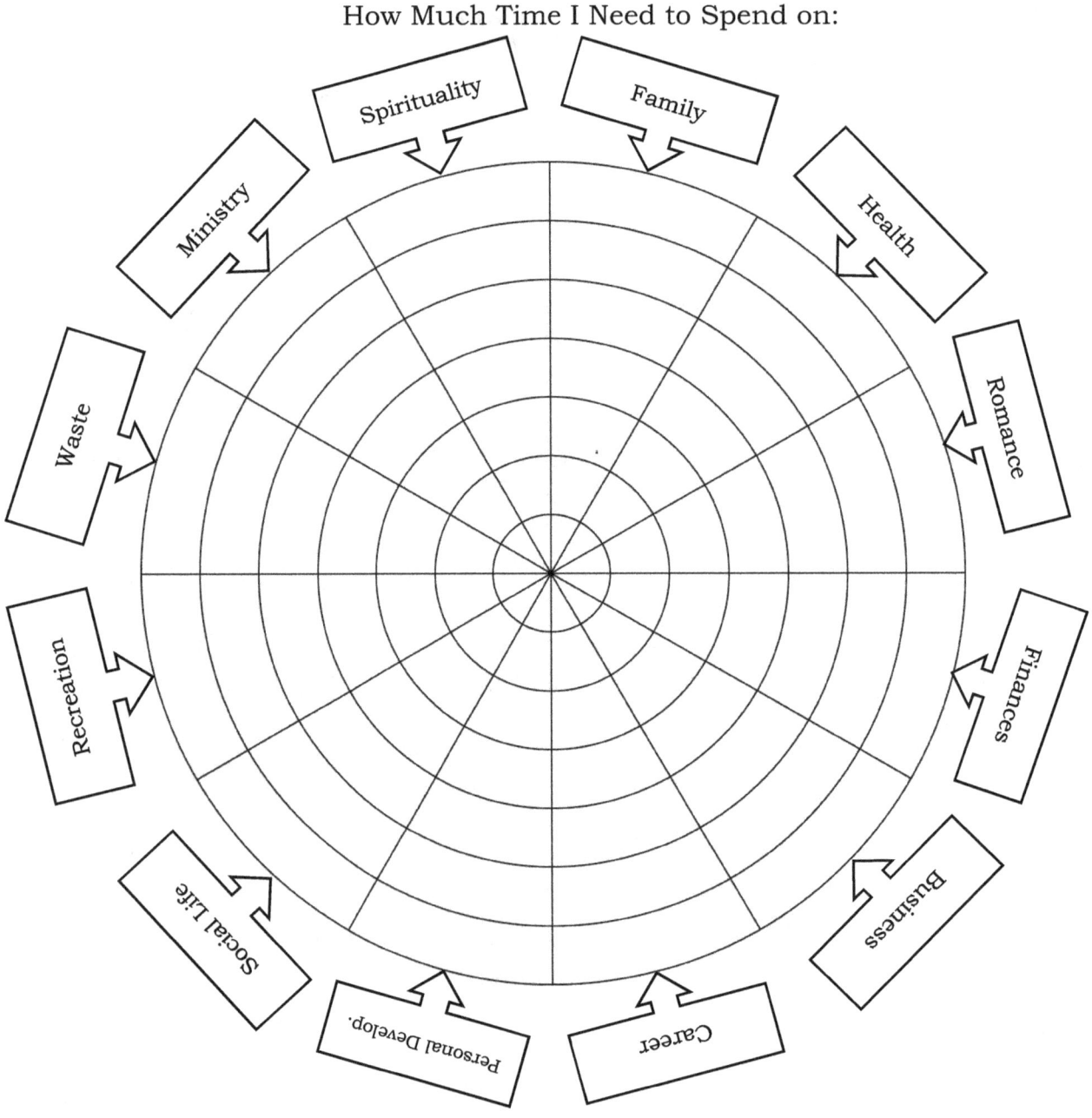

Key 3.7 What areas of helping others bring me the most joy?

No person is an island. We all need each other, which is why it is essential that we develop a lifestyle of helping one another. Philippians 2:4 tells us, "Don't look out only for your own interests, but take an interest in others, too." As we take an interest in others, it is vital that we identify how we are gifted and wired to help others. Those would be the ways that bring us the most joy while we do it. There are times when helping others brings inconvenience or discomfort, but overall, we should walk away with joy knowing that we brought love, life, and light to another person.

The bible says in Acts 20:35, "It is more blessed to give than to receive." Time and time again, the reality of that verse is evident in our lives as we give of our time, talents and resource to others. Different areas of helping others touch each of us differently. Identify your special areas, and target that while being a blessing to others.

Now, you answer: What areas of helping others bring me the most joy?

> Let each of you look not only to his own interests, but also to the interests of others.
>
> Philippians 2:4

Evaluate each statement and mark "T" for true or "F" for false.

☐	I am happiest when I give monetary resources to solve a problem.
☐	I am happiest when I spend time counseling someone.
☐	I am happiest when I create a law or system to correct a problem.
☐	I am happiest when I make others forget about their challenges.
☐	I am happiest when I make other people laugh.
☐	I am happiest when I open my home to people in need.
☐	I am happiest when I serve in my church.
☐	I am happiest when I pray with or for others.
☐	I am happiest when I protect people from dangerous situations.
☐	I am happiest when I provide company for an isolated person.
☐	I am happiest when I volunteer in my community.
☐	I am happiest when I cook for people.
☐	I am happiest when I build things for other people.
☐	I am happiest when I organize events to benefit people.
☐	I am happiest when I travel to poor countries.
☐	I am happiest when I speak publicly.
☐	I am happiest when I clean for people.
☐	I am happiest when I raise awareness about an issue.
☐	I am happiest when I mentor people.
☐	I am happiest when I design things to help people.

Key 3.8 How can I become a solution to a problem that I'm passionate about?

If you see something that is broken, ask yourself, "Can I fix it?" Even if you are not able to completely overhaul or eradicate a problem, evaluate whether or not you can make a significant improvement to it. Chances are, if God has highlighted a problem in your life that you are passionate about, He has also equipped you to address it. Assess what experience, expertise and resources you are able to utilize to make a difference.

Our unique experiences, expertise, and resources help equip us to be the solution to the problems that we have a passion for. No one else has lived your life, and no one else can offer the distinguishing assistance that you were created to give. No one else can reach the people that you can, and no one else can solve the problems that you were created to address in the way that you can.

Now, you answer: How can I become a solution to a problem that I'm passionate about?

_____
_____
_____
_____
_____
_____
_____
_____
_____

Never believe that a few caring people can't change the world. For indeed that's all who ever have.

Margaret Mead

How can I help? Brainstorm 4 different ways you can become a solution to a problem that you're passionate about?

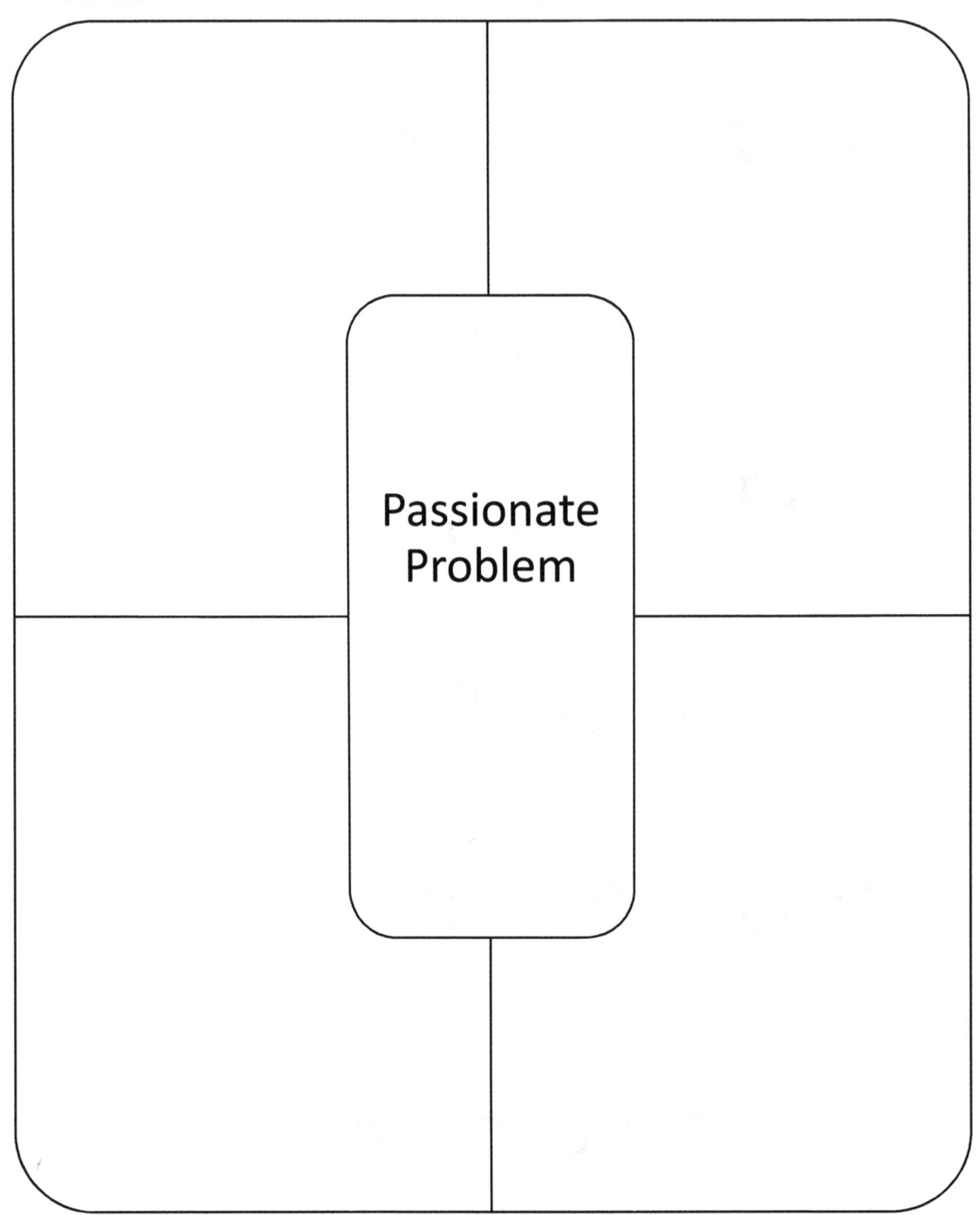

Think Space

This is your space to think, elaborate on a topic, if needed, and write or draw.

Think Space

This is your space to think, elaborate on a topic, if needed, and write or draw.

KEY 4:

DISCOVER PURPOSE IN YOUR POTENTIAL AND PAYMENT

---

po•ten•tial | noun

1. latent qualities or abilities that may be developed and lead to future success or usefulness

pay•ment | noun

1. an amount paid

Key 4.1 What comes naturally for me?

Think about your strengths for a second. If you are one of those people like I used to be, who would only come up with the same three strengths whenever I was probed to reflect on them, try this. Ask ten people for the top ten strengths or abilities that they see in you. The people who see you in action are key players in helping you identify some of those strengths that you may not easily notice. At times, we are too familiar with ourselves and do not even realize that what we naturally do is a desirable attribute that does not come naturally for everyone.

. We all have things that come naturally to us that we may not easily identify because to us, it is just who we are. Reach out to those who know you best to help you identify your strengths. You will most likely begin to see an overlap in the qualities that others see in you.

Now, you answer: What comes naturally for me?
_____
_____
_____
_____
_____
_____
_____
_____
_____
_____
_____
_____

God has given each of you a gift from his great variety of spiritual gifts.
Use them well to serve one another.

1 Peter 4:10-11

Ask five people to identify your top ten strengths, talents and abilities.

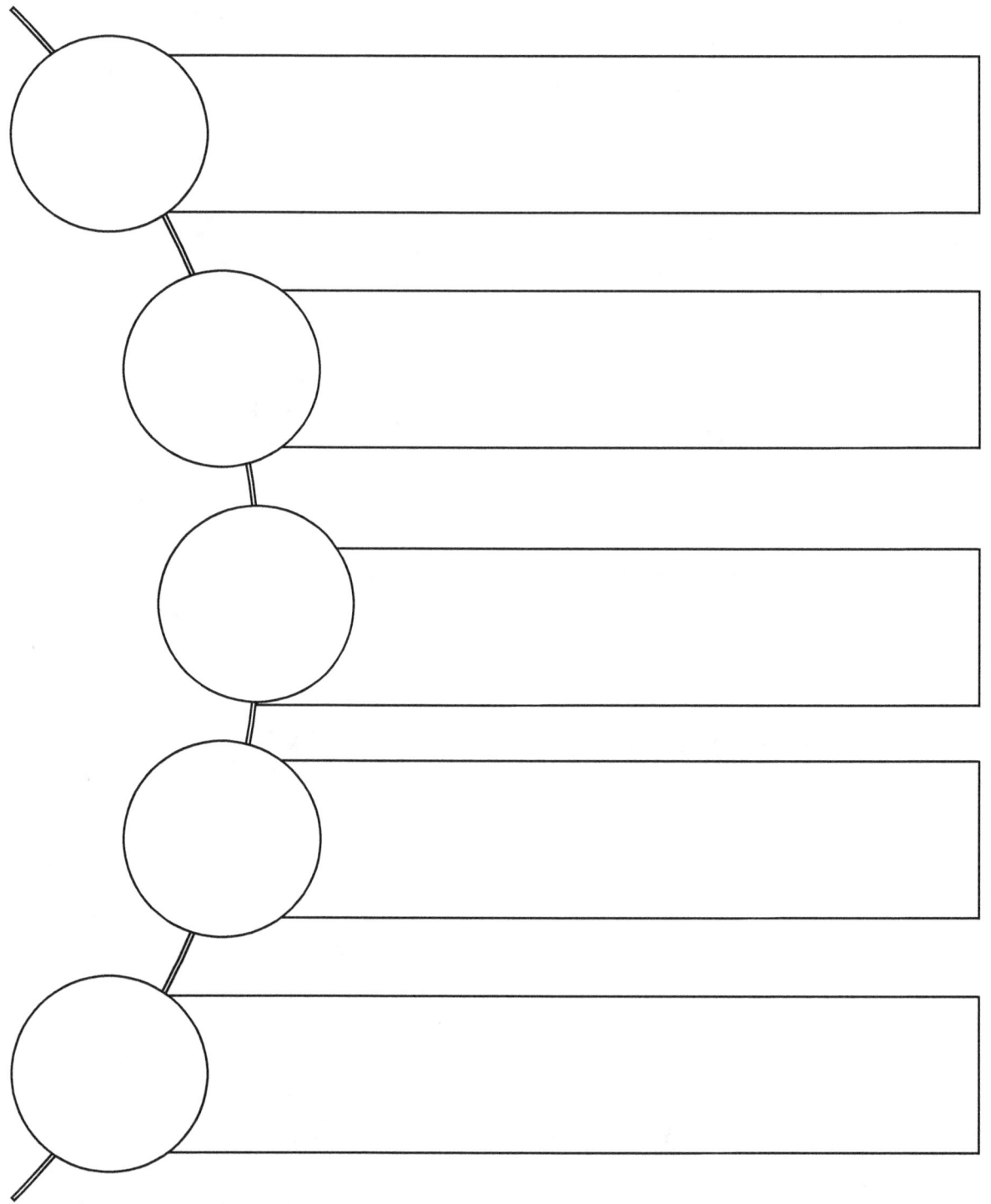

Ask five people to identify your top ten strengths, talents and abilities.

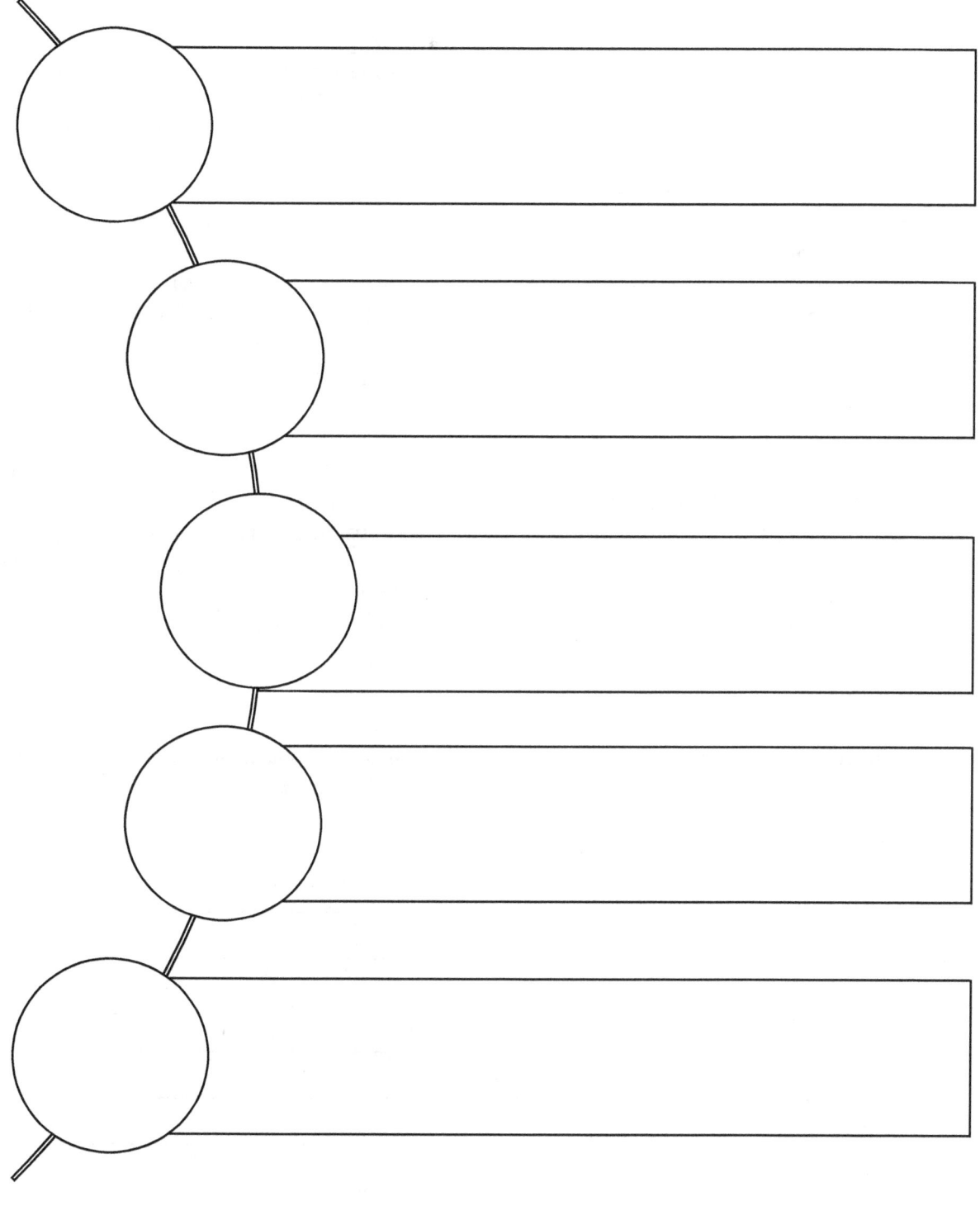

Key 4.2 What motivates me?

What gets you going? What is it that causes you to forget to eat and not want to sleep? Think about the areas as well as the practices that cause you to be all that you can be. A motivator is something that provides a reason or stimulus to do something. Motivators can be intrinsic or extrinsic.

Intrinsic motivators stem from within a person. Either completing an activity is the person's reward, or a person receives personal satisfaction from completing an activity. This is often seen in teachers who make a nominal salary, working almost constant overtime for a thankless job. Their reward is not the prestige or abundant salary, but rather the joys of facilitating children to learn and flourish. Extrinsic motivators are birthed through outside sources. This is when a person completes an activity to receive a reward or avoid a punishment. This is often seen in sales jobs when sales associates fight to meet a quota to avoid negative performance evaluations or to greatly exceed those quotas to be awarded the top salesperson in their department. While both forms of motivation are necessary in various situations, as we strive to reach our fullest potential, intrinsic motivators are ideal and more effective at pushing us to achieve things than their extrinsic counterparts. Think about the intrinsic motivators in your own life. What stimulates you to get it done?

Now, you answer: What motivates me?

_____
_____
_____
_____
_____
_____

People often say that motivation doesn't last. Well, neither does bathing - that's why we recommend it daily.

Zig Ziglar

Check off your motivators.

Achieve Perfection	Facing a Fear	Finding Adventure
Desperation	Justice	Past Trauma
Protecting Others	Repaying a Debt	Peer Pressure
Destiny	Failure	Self- Preservation
Glory	Knowledge	Fitting In
Prove Others Wrong	Revenge	Pleasure
Recognition	To be Remembered	Self-Protection
Money	Fame	Comfort
Avoiding Conflict	Love	Popularity
Greed	Rising Above Others	Curiosity
Prove Yourself	Respect	Freedom
Avoiding Pain	Family	Power
Dominance	Loyalty	Friends
Guilt	Fear	Pride
Rebellion	Morality	Success
Duty	Safety	Thrill
Happiness	Purpose	Attention
Escaping	Not to be Lonely	God
Jealousy	Helping Others	Impatience
Religion	Beauty	Drive

Key 4.3 What is the biggest hindrance that can prevent me from reaching my fullest potential?

When you set out to do anything great, roadblocks and opposition are inevitable. At times, those roadblocks are self-imposed, and at other times they are caused by external factors. Either way, identifying what those roadblocks are and strategically knocking them down is the only way to reach your fullest potential. Know that the roadblocks will come, but you have the ability to knock them down.

Now, you answer: What is the biggest hindrance for me reaching my fullest potential?

_____
_____
_____
_____
_____
_____
_____
_____
_____
_____
_____
_____
_____

Let us strip off every weight that slows us down, especially the sin that so easily trips us up. And let us run with endurance the race God has set before us.

Hebrews 12:1b

Evaluate what is hindering you from reaching your fullest potential. Be sure to follow up and list the date when you overcame the hinderance.

Hinderance:
_____

What can I do to overcome it?
_____
_____

What specifically will it help me to accomplish?
_____
_____

I overcame it on:
_____

Hinderance:
_____

What can I do to overcome it?
_____
_____

What specifically will it help me to accomplish?
_____
_____

I overcame it on:
_____

Hinderance:
_____

What can I do to overcome it?
_____
_____

What specifically will it help me to accomplish?
_____
_____

I overcame it on:
_____

Hinderance:
_____

What can I do to overcome it?
_____
_____

What specifically will it help me to accomplish?
_____
_____

I overcame it on:
_____

Key 4.4 How can I utilize my natural talents, strengths, and motivators to realize the possibilities in my life?

They say if you don't use it, you lose it. With that being said, think about how you can realize your potential by actively cultivating and distributing your talents and strengths. Keep your motivators at the forefront of your mind as you seek to attain every possibility in your life. In Matthew 25, we can see a clear picture of what happens when we fail to utilize what God has given us.

Our gifts are intended to be shared, not hidden, hoarded or distorted. Through prayer, we can seek how God would like us to best utilize our natural talents.

Now, you answer: How can I utilize my natural talents, strengths, and motivators to realize the possibilities in my life?

_____
_____
_____
_____
_____
_____
_____
_____
_____
_____

For we are God's masterpiece. He created us anew in Christ Jesus, so we can do the good things he planned for us long ago.

Ephesians 2:10

Fill in the blanks. Be sure to follow up and list the date when you used your talents to realize the possibilities in your life.

My talent: _____

How can I specifically use it?

_____

What will it help me to accomplish?

_____

I used it on: _____

My talent: _____

How can I specifically use it?

_____

What will it help me to accomplish?

_____

I used it on: _____

My talent: _____

How can I specifically use it?

_____

What will it help me to accomplish?

_____

I used it on: _____

Think Space

This is your space to think, elaborate on a topic, if needed, and write or draw.

Think Space

This is your space to think, elaborate on a topic, if needed, and write or draw.

Key 4.5 What specific costs of my time, energy and resources have I paid to achieve my goals and fulfill my purpose in life and how much am I willing to pay?

I was told that nothing in life is free and I believe it. Our goals are not an exception either. Attaining your goals, reaching your potential and living out your purpose in life will cost you. If you are going to win a prize (which, in this case, is achieving your goals), there is always a price to pay. If you have not paid anything for it, you probably are not reaping the full benefit of the life you can live. It is almost like those free trials of services that companies like to provide to you. You can enjoy it for a limited time with limited features, but if you pay the price, you can enjoy the unending abundance of all they have to offer. Which type of life would you like to live?

Living out your purpose will require your most valuable resource, your time. It will also vie for your energy and other resources. If you want to achieve your goals and fulfill your purpose in life, you will have to pay for it, one way or another—and usually in multiple ways.

Now, you answer: What specific costs of my time, energy and resources have I paid to achieve my goals and fulfill my purpose in life and how much am I willing to pay?

_____
_____
_____
_____
_____
_____

It's not hard to decide what you want your life to be about. What's hard, she said, is figuring out what you're willing to give up in order to do the things you really care about.

Shauna Niequist

Cost Tracker

Label the circle with potential costs. Start at the center of the circle and move towards the outer ring indicating the costs that you have paid to achieve your goals and fulfill your purpose in life. As you allot a greater cost in an area, your shaded area will move closer to the outer ring. Compare the two charts on the next two pages.

Costs of my time, energy and other resources I have paid:

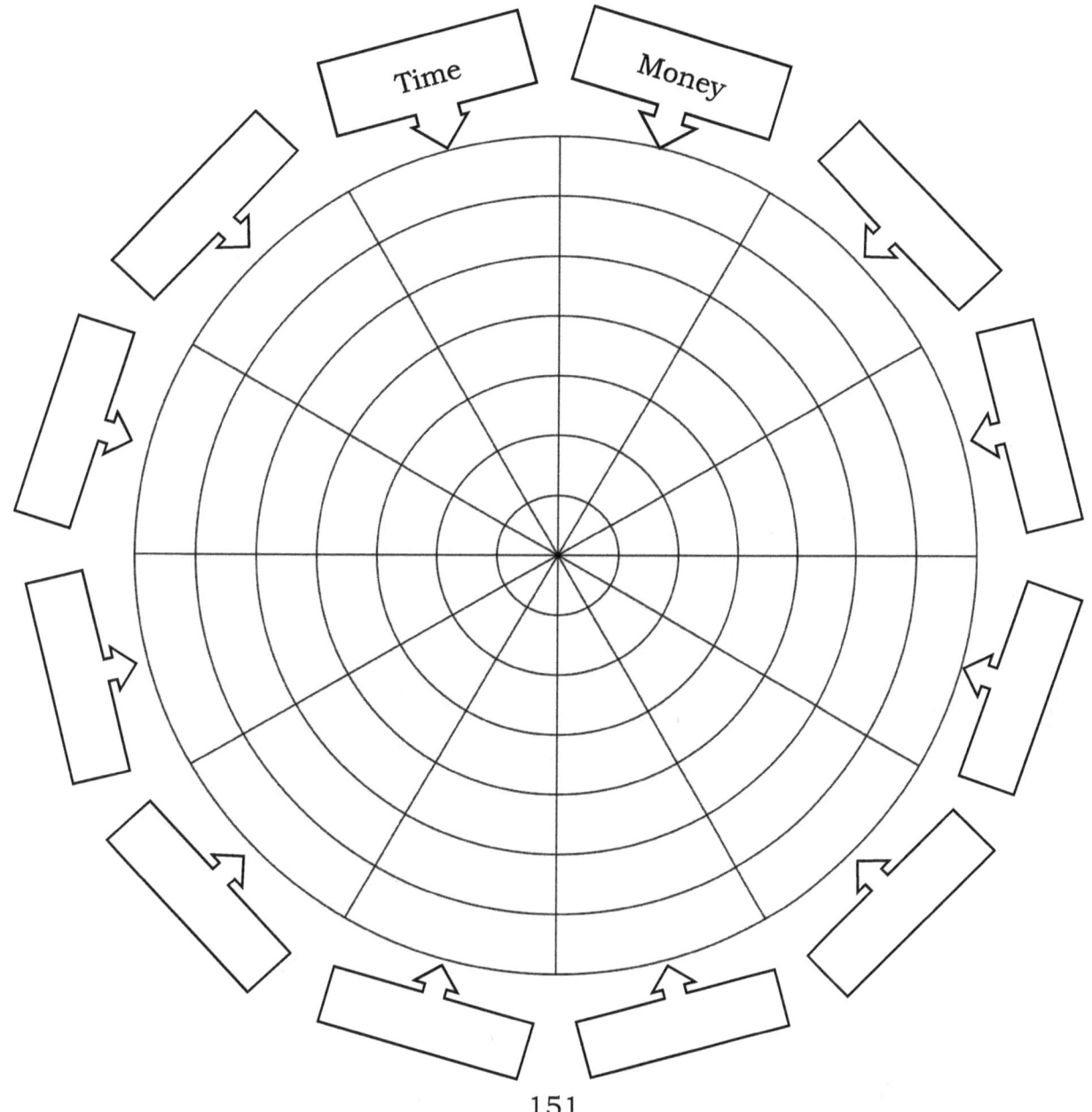

Cost Tracker

Label the circle with potential costs. Start at the center of the circle and move towards the outer ring indicating the costs that you are willing to pay to fulfill your purpose in life. As you allot a greater cost in an area, your shaded area will move closer to the outer ring. Compare the two charts on this page and the previous page.

Costs of my time, energy and other resources I'm willing to pay:

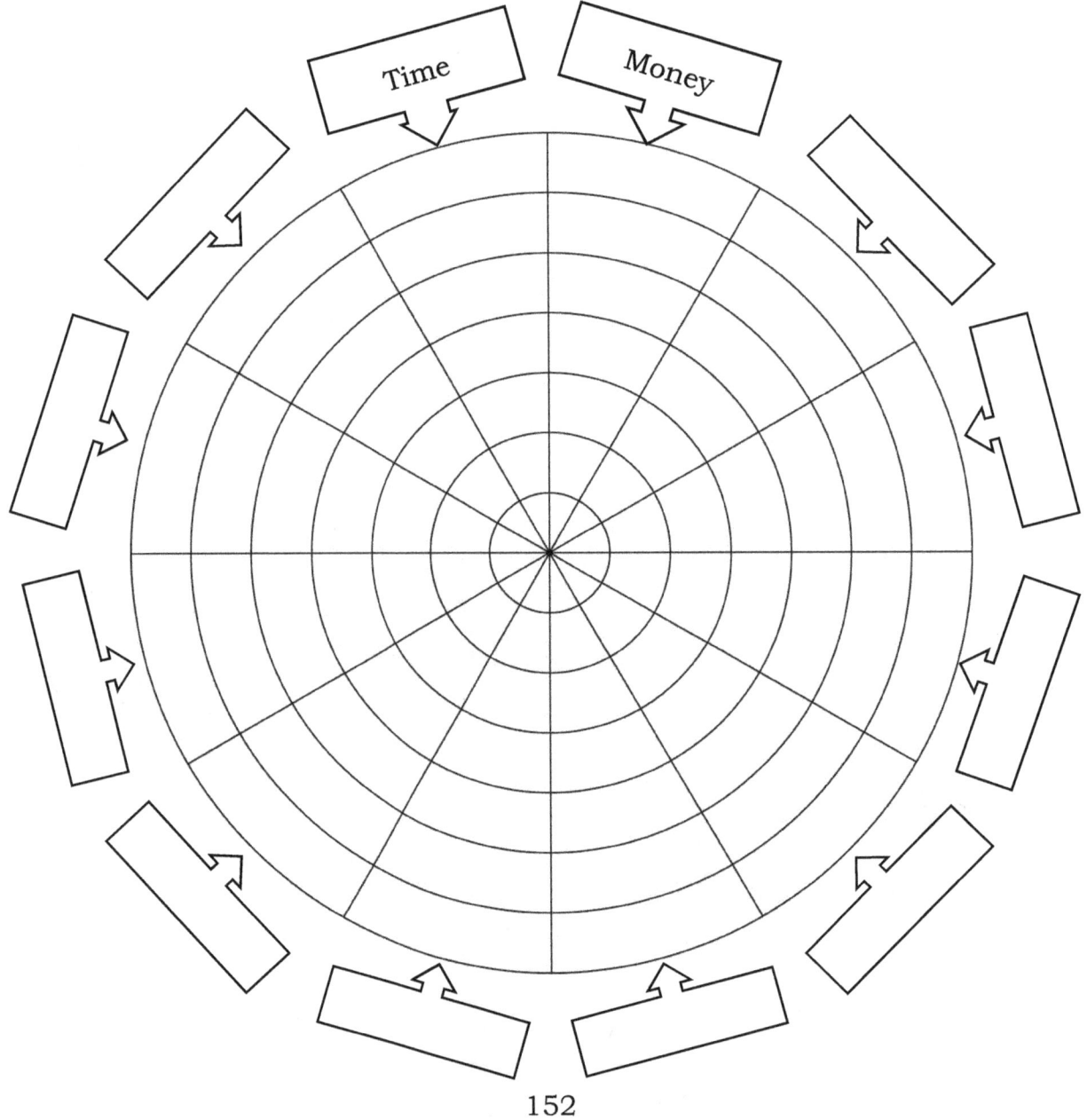

Key 4.6 What am I willing to sacrifice in order to achieve my goals?

Achieving your goals requires a give and take relationship. You are required to give yourself and your resources, and you are also required to let your pursuit of your goals take some things away. It is like the picture of the little girl who had a little teddy bear in her hands. She held on to it tightly with a dismayed countenance as her father requested it from her. He held out his hand to receive the little bear while concealing an even larger bear behind his back to surprise his daughter with. While the sacrifice that we make to achieve our goals will cost us, it will pale in comparison to what we have coming. Unfortunately, we cannot say with certainty how long the time between our sacrifice and achieving our goals will be. We also cannot negate that sacrifice, by definition, is an act of giving up something valued for the sake of something else regarded as more important or worthy.

It is understood that when we sacrifice something, we are acknowledging that the thing that we give up is of value to us but the thing that we are seeking, as a result, outweighs what we give up. Hebrews 12:2 brings this to mind when it says, "Because of the joy awaiting him [Jesus], he endured the cross, disregarding its shame. Now he is seated in the place of honor beside God's throne." Just like Christ, we must look up to what lies ahead in order to lay down what tries to bring us temporary satisfaction in the present. We must be willing to sacrifice in order to achieve our goals.

Now, you answer: What am I willing to sacrifice in order to achieve my goals?

_____
_____
_____
_____

There is no progress or accomplishment without sacrifice.

Idowu Koyenikan

Evaluate each statement and mark "W" for willing to sacrifice or "N" for not willing to sacrifice in order to achieve your goals.

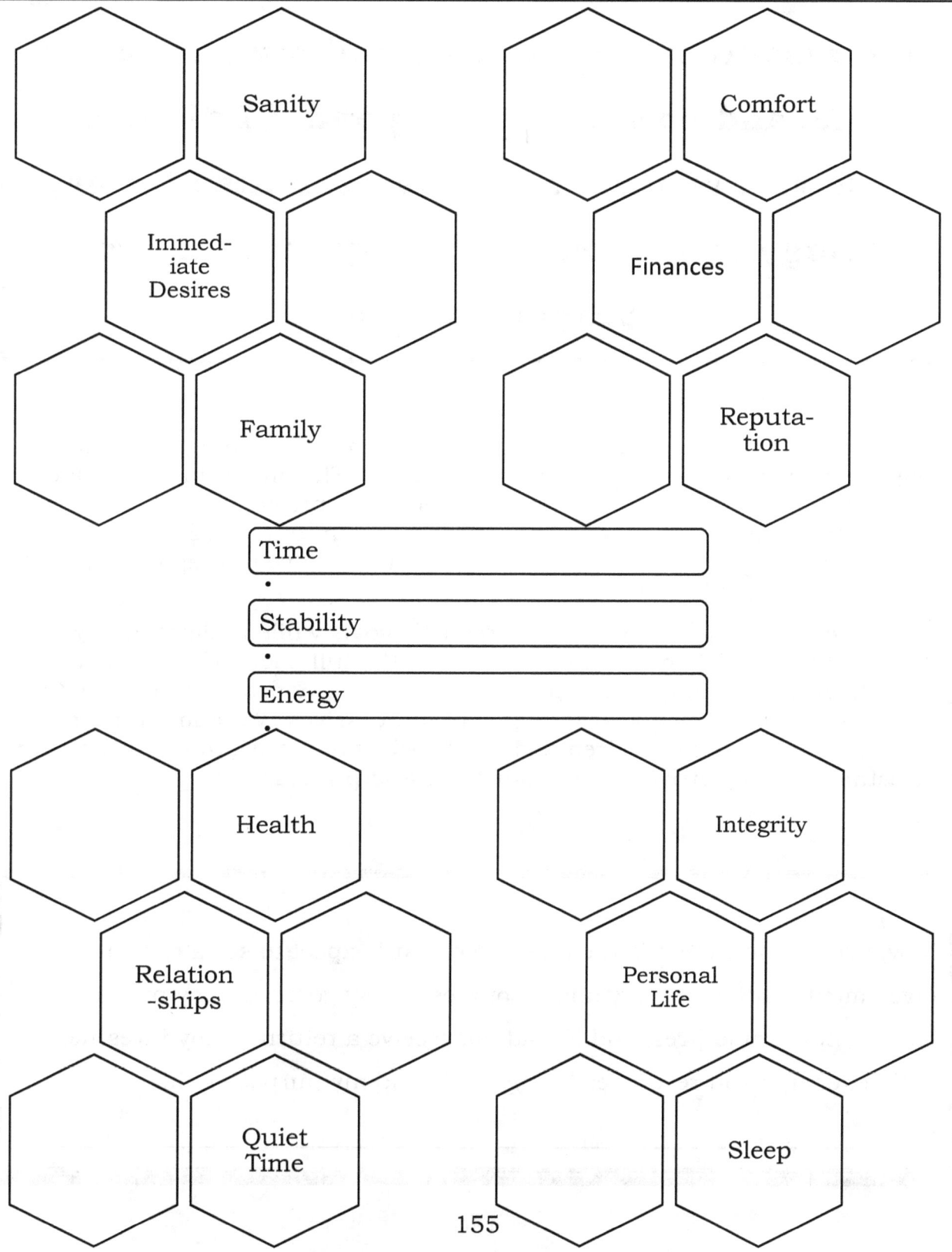

Key 4.7 What is the timeframe that I expect to see a return on my investments of time, energy and resources for my goals and my purpose in life; and how would I respond if I did not receive a return on my investments of time, energy and resources for my goals and my purpose in life?

After we pour our blood, sweat, and tears into something, we expect to reap the benefits of everything that we invested. The only thing is, although we may have a timetable in our minds or a projected return on our investment, we lack the ability to guarantee our outcomes. It is a good measure to set goals and deadlines. It is also imperative to keep in mind that some elements are beyond our control.

In the same way, it is vital to set realistic goals while understanding that there is a possibility that you might not see the full effect of your obedience of walking in your purpose. And that is okay. Our hopes should be that we are a part of something that is bigger than ourselves. We should desire for our children and their children and all of society to receive the return on our investments as we strive towards our goals and purpose in life.

Now, you answer: What is the timeframe that I expect to see a return on my investments of time, energy and resources for my goals and my purpose in life and how would I respond if I did not receive a return on my investments of time, energy and resources for my goals and my purpose in life?

_____

The ultimate test of man's conscience may be his willingness to sacrifice something today for future generations whose words of thanks will not be heard.

Gaylord Nelson

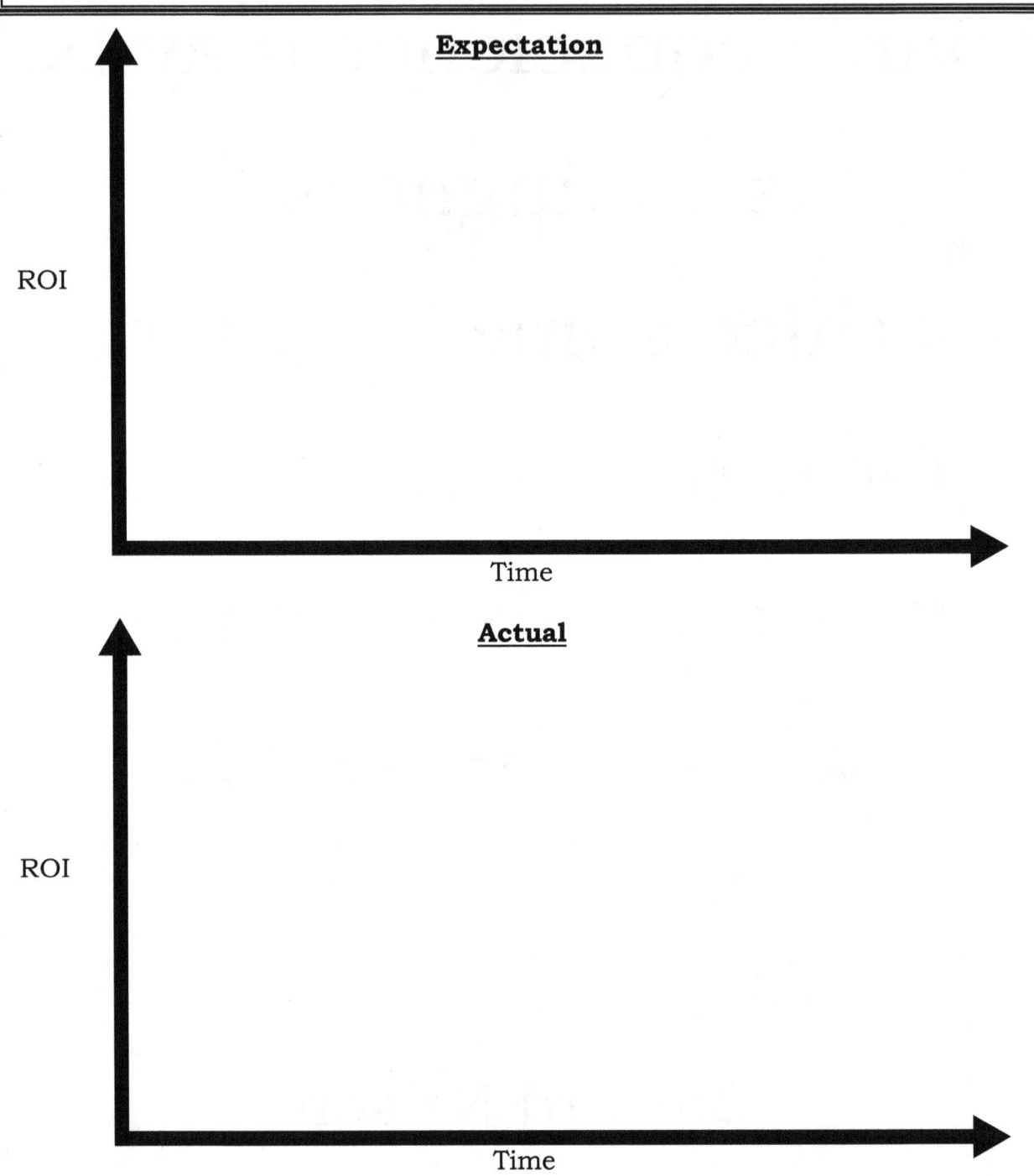

Think Space

This is your space to think, elaborate on a topic, if needed, and write or draw.

Think Space

This is your space to think, elaborate on a topic, if needed, and write or draw.

KEY 5:

PURSUE YOUR PURPOSE

---

pur•sue | verb

1. seek to attain or accomplish (a goal), especially over a long period

pur•pose | noun

1. the reason for which something is created or exists

Key 5.1 Reflect

Reflection is key to growth. Reflection allows you to analyze and assess the overall picture as well as the details of a situation. It allows your mind to wander and your emotions to become free. Reflection works both your mind and heart simultaneously. You are able to ask and answer your own questions for clarity. Two of the best questions that you can ask yourself are, "Why?" and "How?"

The question "Why?" allows you to probe yourself beyond the surface to uncover the root, the motive, the reason behind things that you have done, your response to them and what its lasting effects are. The question "How?" challenges you to take that information and do something with it. It is not enough to recognize the root of a painful experience. The next step is discovering *how* you are going to apply what you learned to improve your future and make a difference.

Throughout this book, you were instructed to answer thirty-four questions about your past, pain, position, posture, personality, passion, potential and payment. Now is the time to reflect on those answers. If you skipped any questions, now is the time to go back to them. If you wrote down a brief thought, now is the time to go back and elaborate on it. Take your time with this step.

Do not be fearful in reflecting. Be open and honest with yourself. I promise that I will not call you up and make you stand before the class and read your responses. This is for your eyes only unless you are comfortable and compelled to share with someone else. The more vulnerable that you are in your reflection, the more beneficial this step will be for you. As you reflect, you may laugh, cry, and have "Ah-ha" moments. Do not hold back. What responses stuck out to you? Embrace it all as you take these steps in pursuing your purpose.

Sometimes, you have to look back in order to understand the things that lie ahead.

Yvonne Woon

Think Space

This is your space to think, elaborate on a topic, if needed, and write or draw.

Mistake Tracker

Don't focus on the mistake. Focus on the time it takes you to identify, learn from and correct the mistake. The shorter the timespan, the better off you are.

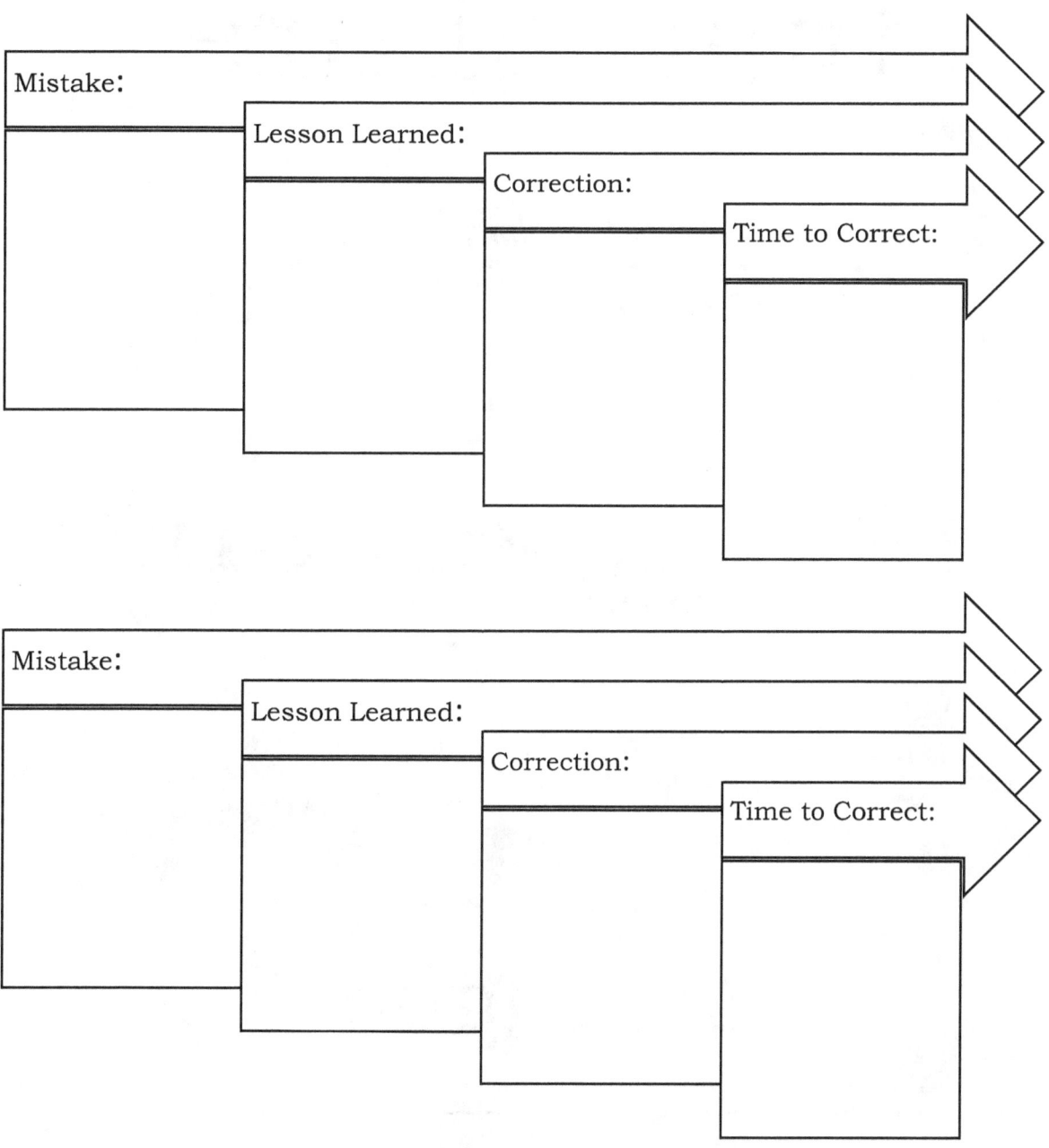

165

> Remember that failure is an event, not a person.
>
> Zig Ziglar

Think Space

This is your space to think, elaborate on a topic, if needed, and write or draw.

Key 5.2 List

After you have reflected on your responses, focus on your responses to the "How can I..." questions throughout each section. These are the blueprints for you to get from where you are to where you need or want to be. For each response, distinguish what your end result is. Next, work yourself backward listing every practical step that you would need to take in order to get to the end result. Your very last step will be your next step that you can realistically take today (or tomorrow if it is late at night.) The purpose in listing your steps is to define realistic bite-sized pieces that you can manage in order to move forward. At times, we see the end result as a vast accomplishment and get petrified by its sheer magnitude and the tons of effort it would require. But if we can break it down and manage many smaller parts of it, we can conquer what initially overwhelms us.

One of the reasons why it took me three years to write the first words or even the outline of *Beauty for Ashes* was that I was gravely intimidated by the idea of writing a *whole* book. Writing an essay, a speech or anything else seemed manageable, but an entire book was too great a task in my mind. When I began to break down my book into bite-sized chunks, I quickly realized that it was not only possible for me to write a book, but the process was much simpler than I ever could have imagined. Now, every time I write a book or coach others along as they write their own books, I start with the end in mind and break down, break down, break down.

If you aim at nothing, you will hit it every time.

Zig Ziglar

The purpose of starting at the end is to see how each step relates to each other. We commonly write down a list of goals but fail to see how each step in our plan aligns with the process of getting from point A to point B. It can be more difficult to figure out what your first step should be than what your last step will be in order to seize your final outcome. Working backward systematically brings your first step right in front of you. It becomes something that you can accomplish immediately.

For example:

My goal for the next three to five years is to homeschool my children in an enjoyable and effective manner that is conducive for them to identify and realize their identity and purpose.

Working backwards from where I need to be to where I am:
1. Homeschool my children in a manner that works, specifically, for our family
2. Be flexible with our curriculum, schedules and practices
3. Connect with other homeschooling families to glean from their practices, resources and experiences
4. Join homeschooling groups and co-operations
5. Research homeschooling options, groups and resources
6. Connect with at least one family who has or is currently homeschooling
7. Call Jane Doe

As you work your way down the list, each step should be an extension of the previous step or answer the question of how you will accomplish the previous step. Once you get to your final step, it should be something that you are able to act on within the next twenty-four hours.

Set GREAT GOALS

G
- **GLORY**
- Does your goal bring **glory** to God?
- Is it ethical?

R
- **REACH**
- Does your goal **reach** other people?
- Does it benefit others?

E
- **EXPLICIT**
- Is your goal **explicitly** stated?
- Is it clear and detailed?

A
- **ASSESS**
- Is your goal able to be **assessed**?
- Can progress be evaluated?

T
- **TIMEFRAME**
- Does your goal have a **timeframe**?
- Does it have a deadline?

How can I apply what I have learned about my past to positively change my present and future? (Reference Key 1.7)

Desired End Result:

_____

My Steps Systematically Working Backwards:

_____
_____
_____
_____
_____

How can I help prevent others from experiencing similar painful experiences as myself or help those who have already experienced similar painful experiences? (Reference Key 1.10)

Desired End Result:

_____

My Steps Systematically Working Backwards:

_____
_____
_____
_____
_____

Think Space

This is your space to think, elaborate on a topic, if needed, and write or draw.

How can I intentionally, positively impact and be impacted by the people who I frequently encounter? (Reference Key 2.5)

Desired End Result:

_____

My Steps Systematically Working Backwards:

_____
_____
_____
_____
_____

How can I allow my attitude, decisions, and reactions to better reflect the impression that I would like to leave with others? (Reference Key 2.9)

Desired End Result:

_____

My Steps Systematically Working Backwards:

_____
_____
_____
_____
_____

Think Space

This is your space to think, elaborate on a topic, if needed, and write or draw.

How can I intentionally put forth the time and effort to get to know myself? (Reference Key 3.3)

Desired End Result:

_____

My Steps Systematically Working Backwards:

_____
_____
_____
_____
_____

How can I become a solution to a problem that I'm passionate about? (Reference Key 3.8)

Desired End Result:

_____

My Steps Systematically Working Backwards:

_____
_____
_____
_____
_____

Think Space

This is your space to think, elaborate on a topic, if needed, and write or draw.

How can I utilize my natural talents, strengths, and motivators to realize the possibilities in my life? (Reference Key 4.4)

Desired End Result:
_____

My Steps Systematically Working Backwards:
_____
_____
_____
_____
_____
_____
_____
_____
_____
_____
_____
_____
_____
_____
_____
_____
_____
_____
_____
_____
_____
_____
_____
_____

Think Space

This is your space to think, elaborate on a topic, if needed, and write or draw.

List your goals for each area.

Spirituality, Family, Health,

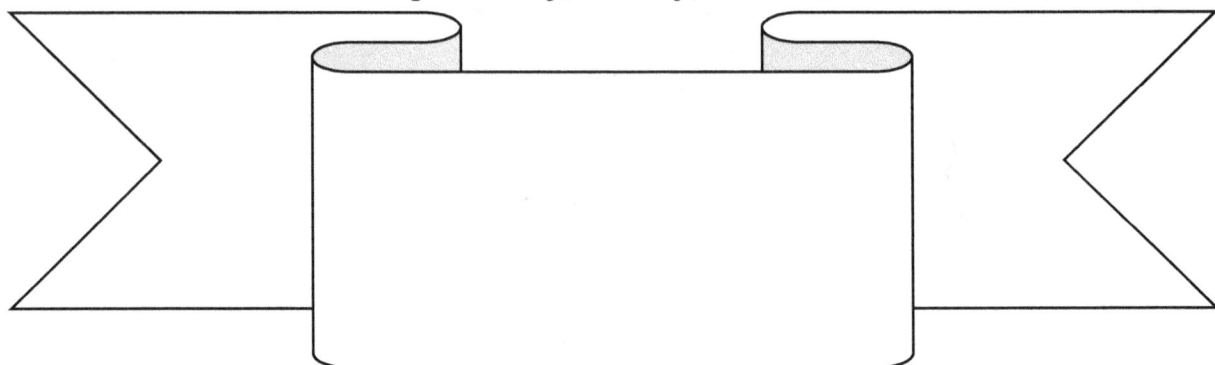

Romance, Finances, Business/Career,

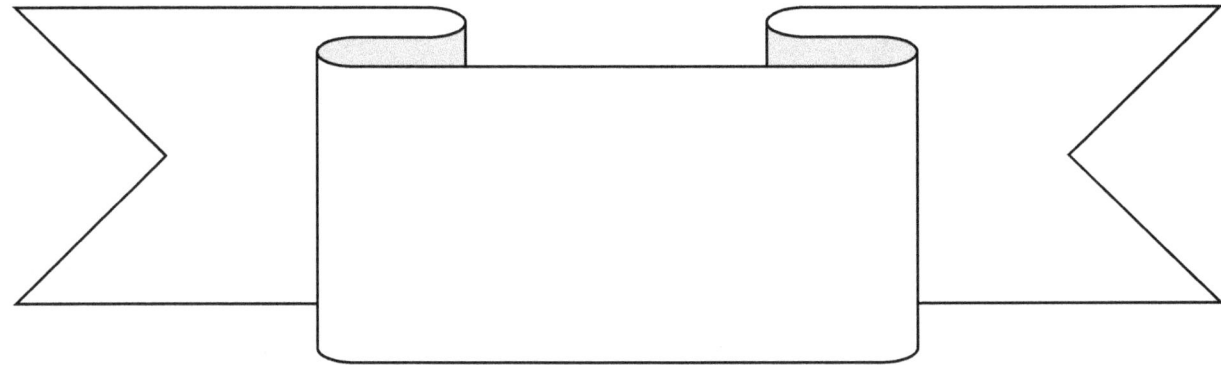

Personal Development, Social Life, Recreation

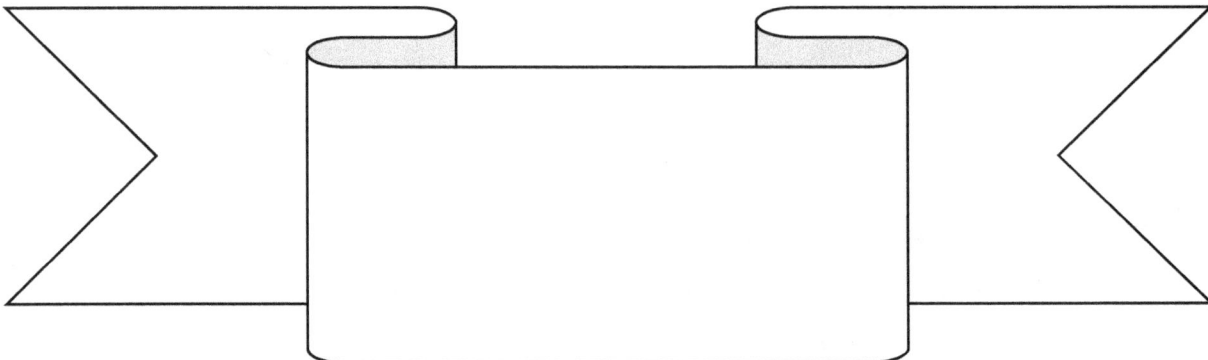

Key 5.3 Share

Once you have listed your goals along with bite-sized steps to achieve them, it is time to begin to share. Sharing is essential to your pursuit of purpose, but it could be detrimental if done incorrectly. Sharing brings a level of accountability and accessibility to the equation. When you share with others, you give them permission to directly or indirectly challenge you and hold you accountable for your words and actions. The key to sharing is to share the *right amount* with the *right people* at the *right time*.

If you want to remember (or be constantly reminded of) anything, tell your children—or any children for that matter. Children are good at bringing your plans back to your remembrance. Of course, I am not suggesting that you should go around telling random children of your plans but do know that once you share it with them, they will innocently check in on you. As I set goals for completing this book, both of my children continued to challenge me, especially if I was playing a game on my phone instead of writing. Hey, I am human, too! I have to admit, having them encourage me and knowing that they were watching my diligence in completing the task motivated me to stay the course.

Outside of motivation is the benefit of wisdom and the accountability factor. When you begin to share your plans with a couple of friends or mentors, you are able to glean wise counsel from those who you know and trust and those who may have walked a similar path. They are able to give you insight and point you to other resources. They also offer support and accountability. Having someone to cheer you on and encourage you, while still challenging you with love is an added bonus. When I was nearing the completion of my book, I had a friend say that she was going to call me the next day to see if I finished the book. She is known for giving me deadlines, and I greatly appreciate her support.

While there is a level of support that sharing with those who are closest to you can bring, there is another dimension that sharing with acquaintances and the public can bring. When you are well established in the foundation of what you are pursuing, I encourage you to reach out to acquaintances and the public. As I wrote this book, I announced its release prior to completing the manuscript. That gave me an added incentive to complete it on time. Share the big picture with anyone who will listen. Always use wisdom and discernment when sharing with others. You will find that those that you least expect to support you could be your biggest supporters. It may be that they are detached enough to appreciate what you are doing without the "Oh, that's just so-and-so" mentality, or maybe they truly have a desire to support your vision. When working on a new project, I reached out to people that I did not talk to in several months, years—or ever. Some people wanted to support me because in the past I helped them when I did not have to. They were grateful for my kindness and wanted to return the favor.

The important thing to note is that when you share, your goal is not to beg, plead or manipulate people into supporting you. You want to give people an opportunity to support you. The right people will rally around you but not if they do not have a clue that you are pursuing whatever your vision or goal is. Sharing also opens the door for networking and collaboration opportunities. Often, sharing what you are pursuing will open the door for much more than what you were expecting. It was through sharing that I became sought after for radio interviews, magazine publications and donations, even when I was not exactly looking out for them at the beginning.

When it comes to judging how much to share, with whom to share it and when to share, always consult God. He knows the hearts of every person. Another thing to keep in mind is that every person that God puts on your heart to seek to connect with will not necessarily be a person with whom you will connect with. It is possible that God allows you to share with particular people who will test your faith and determination in the face of criticism or lack of support. Some of my greatest waves of support were initiated by someone's lack of support. It conditioned my heart and challenged me to depend on God even more. Sharing offers you the benefit of added motivation, support, accountability, networking opportunities, resources and dependence and trust in God.

It takes a lot

of courage

to show

your dreams

to someone else.

Erma Bombeck

Make a note of the benefits you have received from sharing with others the purpose that you are pursuing.

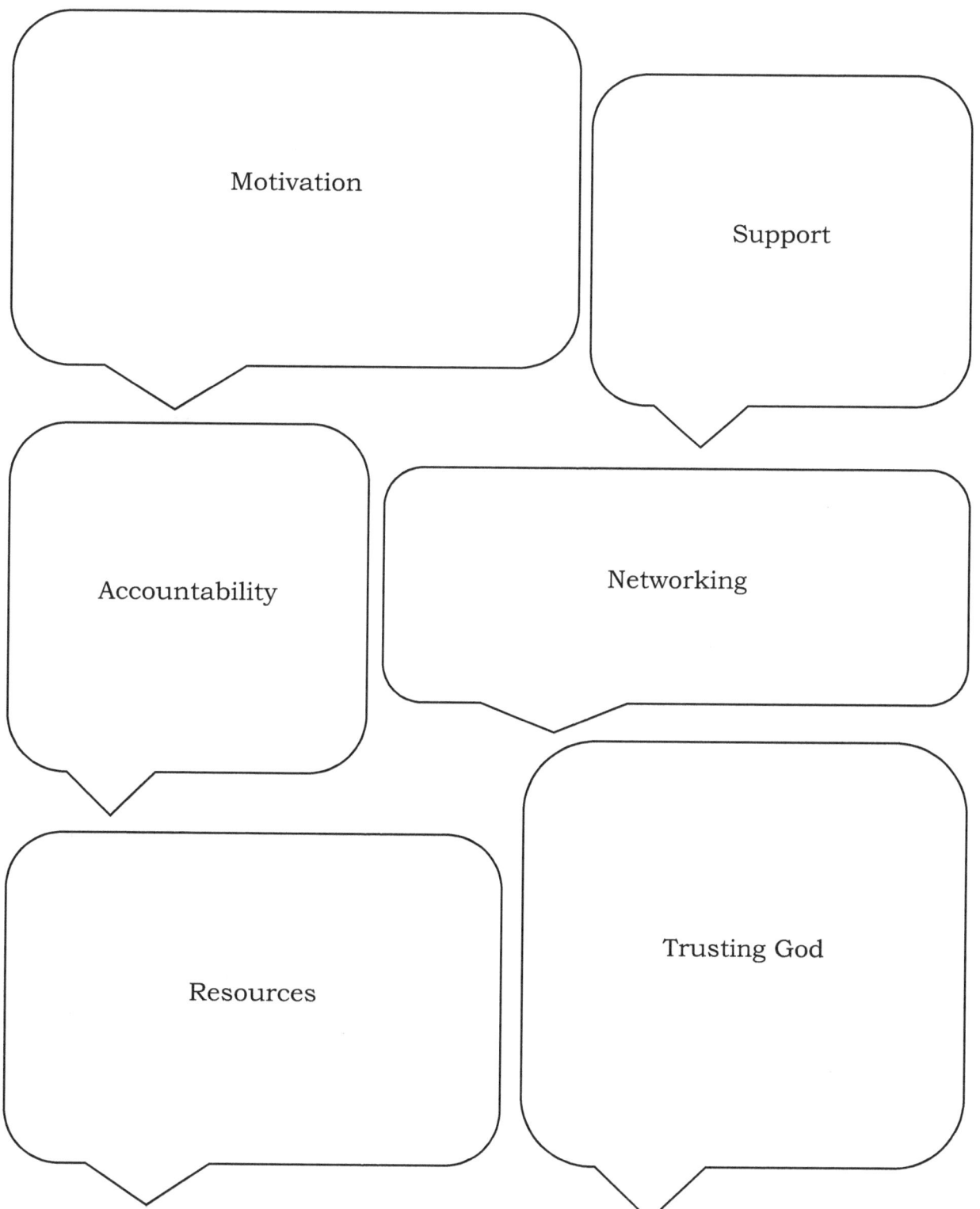

List words of wisdom that you received.

> Two people are better off than one, for they can help each other succeed.

Ecclesiastes 4:9

Key 5.4 Do

This step is a no-brainer. In order to pursue your purpose, you have to actually do something. You can have the greatest ideas and plans in the world, but if you do not act on them, you are simply a dreamer. Why stop at dreaming when you can be an achiever. Being an achiever is greater than achieving your goals for your own selfish ambition. Achievers pave the way for generations to come. Your legacy hinges on your obedience to do what God has placed inside of you to do.

Once you reach this step, it is all about taking those initial steps that you wrote down in the List section (Reference Key 5.2). Whatever is at the bottom of your lists should be steps that you can take within the next twenty-four hours. Do not put it off. Do what you can do today, *today*!

What's at the bottom of your list?
_____
_____
_____
_____
_____
_____
_____

For everything there is a season,

a time for every activity

under heaven...

A time to plant

and a time to harvest...

A time to tear down

and a time to build up...

A time to search

and a time to quit searching.

Ecclesiastes 3:1-6a

If I could continue in the same vein, I would say that there is a time to *plan* and a time to *do*. When you begin to execute your plan, be advised that opposition will come. It is not a matter of if, but rather when. I am reminded of Nehemiah's opposition when he was burdened with the desire to rebuild the walls of Jerusalem. In the fourth chapter of Nehemiah, he depicts the opposition that he faced. His enemies insulted him and his men, tried to stir up trouble against their mission and even attempted to kill them. Look at the diligence, persistence and determination they exuded. Let their example encourage you when opposition comes. Also, take note that Nehemiah could not accomplish his mission alone.

Also our enemies said, "Before they know it or see us, we will be right there among them and will kill them and put an end to the work." When our enemies heard that we were aware of their plot and that God had frustrated it, we all returned to the wall, each to our own work. From that day on, half of my men did the work, while the other half were equipped with spears, shields, bows and armor. The officers posted themselves behind all the people of Judah who were building the wall. Those who carried materials did their work with one hand and held a weapon in the other, and each of the builders wore his sword at his side as he worked. (Nehemiah 4:11, 15b-18)

There is not much more left to be said for this stage. Either you put your plan to work or you settle for leaving this earth with pinned up potential. Your life and the lives that follow you will be fulfilled by the former rather than the latter.

If you can't fly then run, if you can't run then walk, if you can't walk then crawl, but whatever you do you have to keep moving forward.

Dr. Martin Luther King Jr.

Daily Schedule Tracker

What are your priorities?

List them and use them to create your ideal schedule.

Time   Ideal Schedule   Adjusted Schedule

Some things work in theory but not in application. What worked in your initial schedule? Make adjustments, if needed.

Weekly Schedule Tracker

What are your priorities?

List them and use them to create your ideal schedule.

_____
_____

                Ideal Schedule   Adjusted Schedule

Day	Ideal Schedule	Adjusted Schedule
SUNDAY		
MONDAY		
TUESDAY		
WEDNESDAY		
THURSDAY		
FRIDAY		
SATURDAY		

Some things work in theory but not in application. What worked in your initial schedule? Make adjustments, if needed.

_____
_____

Monthly Schedule Tracker

What are your priorities?

List them and use them to create your ideal schedule.

_____

_____

            Ideal Schedule   Adjusted Schedule

	Ideal Schedule	Adjusted Schedule
WEEK 1		
WEEK 2		
WEEK 3		
WEEK 4		
WEEK 5		

Some things work in theory but not in application. What worked in your initial schedule? Make adjustments, if needed.

_____

_____

Habit Checker

It takes about 9 weeks for a habit to become automatic.

Keep track of your progress.

Habit:

	DAY 1	DAY 2	DAY 3	DAY 4	DAY 5	DAY 6	DAY 7
WEEK 1							
WEEK 2							
WEEK 3							
WEEK 4							
WEEK 5							
WEEK 6							
WEEK 7							
WEEK 8							
WEEK 9							

Habit Checker

It takes about 9 weeks for a habit to become automatic.

Keep track of your progress

Habit: _____

	DAY 1	DAY 2	DAY 3	DAY 4	DAY 5	DAY 6	DAY 7
WEEK 1							
WEEK 2							
WEEK 3							
WEEK 4							
WEEK 5							
WEEK 6							
WEEK 7							
WEEK 8							
WEEK 9							

Key 5.5 Check

Whether you are in school, employed or pursuing your purpose, evaluating where you are and how you are doing is essential. During this stage, you want to assess where you are in the grand scheme of your purpose. Do not only look at how many things you have checked off of your list of things to do but also your effectiveness and the outcomes of completing those tasks. Evaluate your own strengths and weaknesses throughout the process.

Checking to see how things are going is not a one-time task. As you progress through the process of pursuing your purpose, you should periodically conduct evaluations. When I first wrote the business plan for my women's ministry, Secure and Complete, I sat on it. I was empowered and on fire to check that item off my list of things to do, but then my momentum faltered. I was not consistently making strides in the direction of my goals. Checking in allows you to assess whether or not you are consistently moving forward.

The success of continually checking items off of your list can be invigorating, but it cannot stop there. You have to go a step further and evaluate how successful the strides that you are making are to the overall purpose that you are pursuing. The last thing you want to do is to occupy your time, energy, and resources with futile tasks. Do not be a *Martha* when you can be a *Mary*.

As Jesus and the disciples continued on their way to Jerusalem, they came to a certain village where a woman named Martha welcomed him into her home. Her sister, Mary, sat at the Lord's feet, listening to what he taught. But Martha was distracted by the big dinner she was preparing. She came to Jesus and said, "Lord, doesn't it seem unfair to you that my sister just sits here while I do all the work? Tell her to come and help me." But the Lord said to her, "My dear Martha, you are worried and upset over all these details! There is only one thing worth being concerned about. Mary has discovered it, and it will not be taken away from her" (Luke 10:38-42).

Distraction Tracker

What are the things that are getting you off task from pursuing your purpose and achieving your goals?

Distraction   Frequency

	HOURLY	DAILY	2-3X WEEK	WEEKLY	MONTHYLY	YEARLY

All of your efforts should be purposeful and contribute to your end goal. At times, the contribution that a particular task will make is simply showing you what not to do. When you have those moments, treasure them because they may, in fact, be more valuable than the things that you do correctly. When I used a publisher for my first book, I ran into some challenges. Instead of pouting about it when things did not pan out the way that I expected, I captured those instances as learning opportunities. Those very challenges became prominent points in my mind as I began to build my own publishing company, Glorious Works Publishing.

Lastly, remember to check yourself. Assess the areas that you are excelling in and the areas that you could use more work in. Sometimes it may not be an intellectual deficiency. It could be a mental or behavioral adjustment that you need to make. You could notice that if you do not set a strict schedule that you do not accomplish your goals. It could be vice versa, where you notice that strict schedules detract from your overall productivity. As you evaluate yourself, remember that you are human, so be kind to yourself.

You would not find it acceptable for your employer to fail to evaluate your performance, so do not accept it from yourself. The benefit of checking in on your progress is valuable and should be taken advantage of consistently. It helps you to gauge where you are going by assessing where you are.

Evaluate what's working and what's not working.

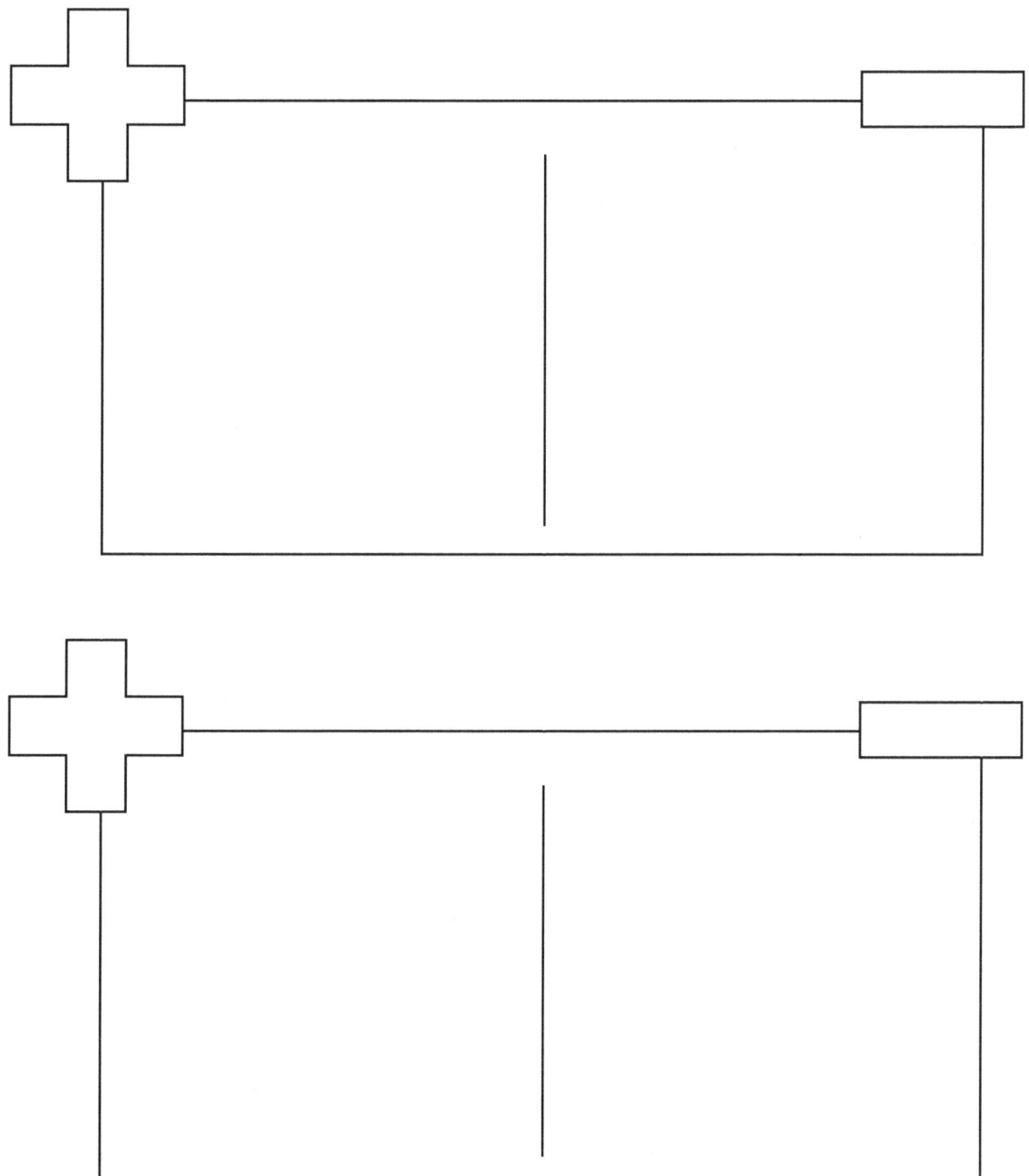

Evaluate the areas in which you are excelling and struggling.

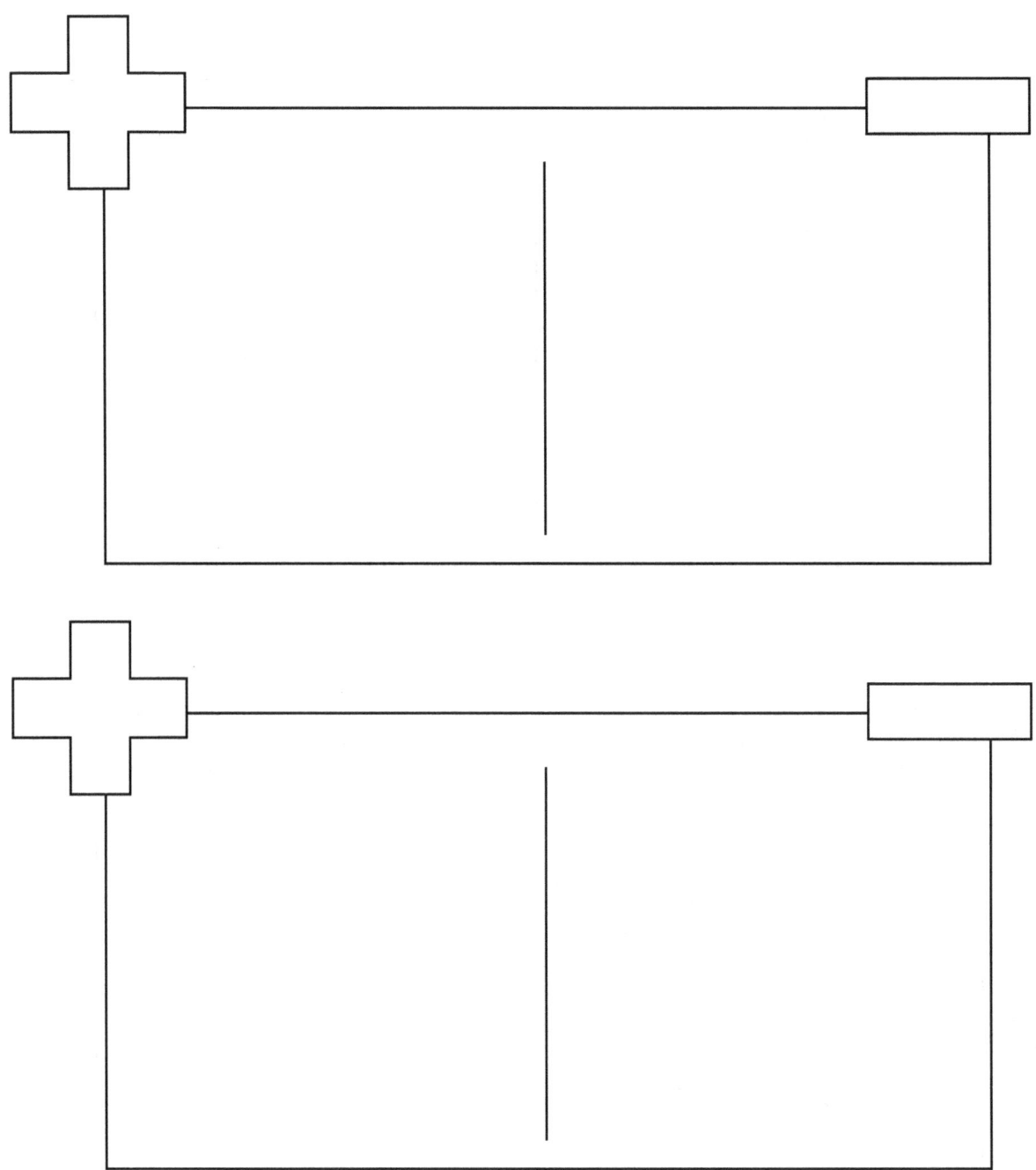

Key 5.6 Repeat

You did it! You accomplished that goal; you changed your career; you started your business; you wrote your book; you started your family; you led that ministry; you moved to that country; you received that degree. Now what? As you know, life goes on after you attain a goal or milestone. The beauty is that we were not created for a singular purpose, which once we discover and fulfill, that is it, we can now put our feet up and just glide aimlessly through the rest of our life. Wrong! That's not our original design.

Often when we hear people talk about discovering purpose or pursuing purpose, they say it as if it is only one thing. The truth is that we were created with purposes and our purposes are multifaceted. I believe there is an overarching purpose that we are all called to, which is to glorify God and to make disciples of Jesus Christ, but the way in which we carry out those purposes are unique to us. In every season and every situation, God has a purpose for us. When your car breaks down purely so that you can have a life-changing conversation with the mechanic, that is purpose being fulfilled. The key is to be able to recognize that purpose in every area of your life and maximize your opportunities to actively pursue it.

Throughout this book, you were able to discover purpose in your past, pain, position, posture, personality, passion, potential and payment. Each of those areas is essential. God can and wants to use every part of you—the good, the bad, the ugly and indifferent. As you continue to live out your purpose in life, periodically repeat these steps. Life's experiences and incremental knowledge have a way of changing our perspectives. What may have applied to you at one particular point in your life could drastically change at another point. As long as you are living, continue pursuing purpose.

CONGRATULATIONS

_____

(Name)

ON

PURSUING YOUR PURPOSE

DATE: _____

SIGNED: KYRA LANAE

CONTINUE PURSUING PURPOSE UNTIL YOU FINISH THE RACE.

"I HAVE FOUGHT THE GOOD FIGHT,

I HAVE FINISHED THE RACE,

AND I HAVE REMAINED FAITHFUL."

2 TIMOTHY 4:7

ABOUT THE AUTHOR

The question of *why* Kyra Lanae does what she does is more important than the question of *who* she is. Kyra Lanae's relationship with Jesus Christ and desire to please her Father, God, is the driving force behind everything she does. Whether writing books, speaking publicly, mentoring or encouraging others in her daily life, her heart's desire is to help people. As for *who* she is, Kyra Lanae is a Christ-follower and mother native to Philadelphia, Pennsylvania. Kyra Lanae currently resides in the Philadelphia Suburbs with her two wonderful children, Cameron Nasir and Sabrina Marie.

Kyra Lanae is an internationally known author, publisher, and dynamic, inspirational, and authentic speaker who empowers women worldwide in the areas of identity, purpose, relationships, parenting, ministry and writing. Kyra is the author of *Beauty for Ashes: The Transformation of my Life's Darkest Moments* and *Pursuing Purpose: 5 Keys to Fulfilling Your God-Given Purpose*. Kyra is also the founder and president of Glorious Works Publishing.

Kyra delivers wisdom and practical application as she shares her successes and failures transparently. Kyra is wise beyond her years which enables her to relate to women of all ages from Millennials to Baby Boomers. When she writes or speaks, you are sure to walk away with a new perspective, unearthed courage or reasonable next steps. She is like a gold miner of the heart, digging up precious treasures in the women whom she addresses. As women's identities, mindsets, and lives are transformed, so are their families, ministries, careers, businesses and communities. As Kyra pours strength into women, she motivates them to continue the cycle of strengthening other women. Women glean from the faith, hope and love that Kyra exudes as she walks women through her journey of overcoming rape, divorce, addictions and suicidal thoughts, just to name a few, and pursuing her God-given purpose in life.

Kyra Lanae has had the honor of being featured in *31 Wife in Training*, an international Christian Women's magazine based out of Cape Town, South Africa. Kyra has also been a special guest and speaker for ministries and organizations including Gathering Connection Fellowship, Simplicity HealthStyle and CareerGPS. Kyra's refreshing spirit, wisdom, influence and contribution has opened the door for recurring invitations from every organization with whom she has partnered.

Kyra Lanae can be reached via email at admin@kyralanae.com or directly through her website, kyralanae.com. For booking, please visit kyralanae.com/booking. For publishing, please visit gloriousworkspublishing.com.

More Titles by Kyra Lanae

Beauty for Ashes: The Transformation of my Life's Darkest Moments

Pursuing Purpose: 5 Keys to Fulfilling Your God-Given Purpose

Coming Soon by Kyra Lanae

Oh, the Things That They Say: Life Lessons to Learn From the Silly Things That Kids Say

Moment by Moment Journal: Living Life After Losing a Loved One

Life Lessons for Kids Series: Will You Play With Me?

Purely Single: How to Successfully and Enjoyably Experience Purity and Singleness

www.ingramcontent.com/pod-product-compliance
Lightning Source LLC
Chambersburg PA
CBHW080336170426
43194CB00014B/2587